How Boys Become Men

HOW BOYS BECOME MEN

Transforming Dragon Spirit into
Courageous Heart

Ted Braude

 GOLDENSTONE PRESS | *Benson, North Carolina*

Published by Goldenstone Press
P.O. Box 7
Benson, North Carolina 27504
www.goldenstonepress.com

ISBN: 978-0-9832261-6-1

Cover artwork: *Gawain Discovers Hautdesert*
by Simon Schmidt
http://alarie.ce/

Cover and book design: Eva Leong Casey/Lee Nichol

Printed in USA

GOLDENSTONE PRESS

GOLDENSTONE PRESS seeks to make original spiritual thought available as a
force of individual, cultural, and world revitalization. The press is an integral
dimension of the work of the School of Spiritual Psychology. The mission of the
School includes restoring the book as a way of inner transformation and awakening to spirit. We recognize that secondary thought and the reduction of books to
sources of information and entertainment as the dominant meaning of reading
places in jeopardy the unique character of writing as a vessel of the human spirit.
We feel that the continuing emphasis of such a narrowing of what books are
intended to be needs to be balanced by writing, editing, and publishing that em-
phasizes the act of reading as entering into a magical, even miraculous spiritual
realm that stimulates the imagination and makes possible discerning reality from
illusion in the world. The editorial board of Goldenstone Press is committed to
fostering authors with the capacity of creative spiritual imagination who write
in forms that bring readers into deep engagement with an inner transformative
process rather than being spectators to someone's speculations. A complete cata-
logue of all our books may be found at *www.goldenstonepress.com*. The web page
for the School of Spiritual Psychology is *www.spiritualschool.org*.

10 9 8 7 6 5 4 3 2 1

For Tom Fitzpatrick and Nori Braude

CONTENTS

~ �֎ ~

Change is moving from the known to the unknown.

— Joseph Chilton Pearce

ACKNOWLEDGEMENTS

This book is entirely possible from the love, encouragement, and generous support of Daniel and Nori Braude. I am deeply grateful to them.

My deepest appreciation to Robert Sardello and the School of Spiritual Psychology for recognizing the qualities hidden in boys becoming young men, and the alchemical magic of parents in their boys becoming the men they were born to become.

I must acknowledge the presence and participation of the Men's Council as a bedrock of support, courage, and commitment.

Kevin Meisel, master artist, pursuer of truth, love, and beauty.

Rob Wachler, the standard-bearer of commitment.

Howard Schubiner, trailblazer and devotee of kindness.

Craig Daly, an extraordinary friend of remarkable courage.

Michael Baldridge, the Cap'n of intelligence and order.

Ainars Pavlovics, the master of rules who cares with a boundless heart.

D. Spencer Price, the grand fire-master who creates light and heat with enormous generosity.

Tim McDonald, whose vision and ferocious love keeps me on track.

John Hammond's friendship and confidence in BoysWork over many years helped give birth to the book. Before its conception, he threw his life into the video project that visualizes moving from dragon spirit to courageous heart.

Mitch Jacobs, my twin brother from a different mother, has nurtured all the seeds that bore the fruit that is this book.

Fred and Roz Lessing recognized and brought along the man who was becoming from the boy that was me.

I rest in the arms of Madame Pink's love that knows no boundaries. Words cannot convey the welcoming presence of her soul in my life. Her love, in form and action, infuses this work.

Gwendolyn and Mirabeth Braude have listened to me talk about boys for years, and share the intention that boys become men.

Gerald Braude read, commented on, and encouraged an early draft of the book.

My sincere appreciation to Lee Nichol for his editing mastery, Eva Casey for her artistry and design, and Paolo Catalla for his illustrations of the physical movements and gestures.

I must recognize the individuals and institutions who have believed in BoysWork and the vision of boys becoming young men, including, but not limited to:

      Gordon Clay and Menstuff.org
      Sr. Bridget Bearss and the Academy of the Sacred Heart
      Joanne Swan-Jones and the Corpus Christi School
      Julie Fisher and Building Better Families in Action
      Partnership for Dads

Connie Doherty and the Troy Public Library
Paul Linden and Aiki-Extensions
John Callaghan
Karen Moss
Kathe Koja
The Northville Group
Byron and Catherine

My heartfelt gratitude to all the parents, teachers, administrators, counselors, librarians, social workers, juvenile court personnel, and other adults interested in the welfare of boys who have heard versions of the book in public presentations.

Lastly, and very importantly, I take my hat off to the boys who have taught me well and whose stories inform and grace these pages. I cannot thank you enough!

INTRODUCTION

I want to stop things at seventeen or eighteen, just before high school graduation. That would be perfect. I can drive, go wherever I want, be around my friends, but not have to be responsible for anything. Not have to work and support myself. Working and being responsible: that would suck.

—13-year-old boy

I don't know what it is to be a man. Or how to become one. When I look forward, I don't like what I see and I don't know what I can do about it. I'm stuck.

—18-year-old boy

There is a long, colorful history of teenage boys acting disruptive, obnoxious, obstinate, disobedient, reclusive, reckless, and withdrawn. An equally long historical explanation fits with the theme of *How Boys Become Men: From Dragon Spirit to Courageous Heart*— teenage boys are "men-in-the-making" who require both a cultural context of manhood, and training to become the men they were born to become. That training is always in the form of "a hero's journey," ultimately leading the boy to discovering and living his purpose as a man, and preparing to fulfill his soul's destiny. But if there is no cultural context for this training, the journey is lost.

In the absence of a culturally accepted model of manhood and effective initiation rites of passage, boys are languishing in adolescence well into their late twenties and early thirties. This shows in a lack of ambition and motivation, fear of risks and completing tasks, withdrawal into entertainment and fantasy, poor school performance, low confidence, little integrity, and substance abuse. Often, the boys who make it out of high school and through college try to move on to "the next step" feeling lost, with no direction or purpose, and aching to join "the fight club" so they can feel strong and potent.

Parents are at a loss with what to do with their teenage sons. They find themselves constantly trying to get them to change. The result is incessant arguing, fighting, opposition, anguish, misery, and frustration. This produces zero maturation. In fact, both "trying to get them to change" and "letting them do their own thing" enables boys' lack of growth and development. Neither approach has the necessary ingredients they need to become young men.

This condition is equally frustrating for the boys: they are ripe for an engagement and a context that enables them to mature. *How Boys Become Men* provides this engagement and context. It gets to the very root of the dynamics of power, conflict, and love that are the foundation for developing maturity, confidence, integrity, and purpose.

I have worked as a therapist with boys and their families for over thirty years. Once, I mentioned in a clinic staff meeting that I would work with teenage boys, and I practically got a standing ovation! They're not a clientele therapists usually like to work with. Teenage boys are generally viewed by clinicians (and grown-ups in general) as "a problem" to be "fixed." Their behavior certainly reinforces that viewpoint. Yet, I've always found their actions interesting, engaging, and communicative: a kind of code which, once it's been deciphered, opens the door to authentic growth and development.

Outside of the office, I have run groups with boys and consulted with schools in developing boy-friendly education programs, supervising their staffs, and training their boys. I've presented workshops and programs for boys, parents, educators, youth assistance workers, librarians, criminal justice personnel, and other professionals.

For more than fifteen years, I've given what I call "dragon-taming" presentations to parent groups in conferences, community centers, parent education programs, and drug prevention programs throughout southeastern Michigan. In each presentation, I ask parents, "What is on your minds . . . what's concerning you about your sons?" Invariably, the question I get is, "Why doesn't he just do what he's suppose to do? It would be so much easier." That's only the beginning.

There are always what I refer to as the "fire-breathing" questions, including: "Why does he argue and fight with me (and/or his other parent or siblings)?" "Why does he swear so much?" "Why is he so loud or shouting?" There are also the "cave dweller" questions: "Why does he stay in his room all of the time?" "Why does he ignore me?" "Why doesn't he talk with me/us anymore?"

Parents always ask about attitude and behavior: "Why is he so lazy?" "Why doesn't he have interest or passion in anything?" or "All he cares about is _____ ?" and the universal "Why does he leave his stuff all over the place?" There are questions about the computer, video games, social networking, and texting too.

Without fail, parents ask about school: "Why doesn't he do his homework?" "Why doesn't he get better grades?" "Why doesn't he turn in his homework after he's done it?!" Finally, the grand pair that brings all parents to their knees: "Why can't I get him to _____ ?" and "Why does he push my buttons?!"

As the questions fly, there is a room full of heads nodding, frowns and smiles facing each other, and nervous laughter accompanied by occasional bellows. Inside of all the parents' concerns are more questions that are never asked. They've lost touch with their sons: he's growing up, getting bigger, identifying more with friends or peers, or in reverse becoming more isolated from peers, but coming no closer to his family. They do not know what to do with him: they're stuck.

All of their questions can be answered easily once parents understand the world of a teenage boy. Once they have "knowledge of the beast," things become much clearer. Their lives change dramatically when parents learn the dynamics of power, conflict, and love, and put them into practice in the ways that fit with what their "dragon" needs developmentally to grow into a young man.

I'm often asked, "Where does the dragon idea (in the book's subtitle) come from?" It began intuitively. I needed a title for a talk I was planning on teenage boys and "taming the dragon" popped into my head. It occurred to me that in *The Hobbit* is the idea that dragons are dangerous whether they're awake or asleep. Awake, they're ready to attack intruders or destroy anyone they come into contact with, and when they're "asleep," they're "dreaming" up their next conquest. I knew intuitively that this was a fitting description for teenage boys. The "dragon" idea spawned an entire metaphoric imagery to present to parents: "knowledge of the beast" being the world of a teenage boy, "fire-breathing" referring to loud, disruptive, swearing, confrontational behavior, "cave-dwelling" equaling silent, removed, isolated, hiding out in his room, and "soft underbelly" to be the open, vulnerable condition of the boy.

My imagination progressed when I realized that boys and parents fighting with each other week after week in my office was nothing more than stirring the pot: a lot of noise, emotion, and activity but no power—no change. As a second-degree black belt in the Japanese martial art Aikido, I've learned to sense and watch movement, the flow of *ki*—the invisible life force flowing through and around physical matter, informing its actions. These family fights were nothing more than an energetic eddy swirling around going nowhere. There is no real power. In Aikido, one learns to ally with the flow of *ki*, the direction of action, to blend with and re-direct it. I applied this principle and practice with boys and their parents. The result: power became present as a quality beyond control and domination, and change occurred. The light bulb went off in my head: this is what the boys are fighting about! They're trying, unknowingly, to provoke a change for themselves and their families through the activities they're masters at: games and fights. The change they need creates more maturity for them and more love for everyone. In fact, I recognized, boys feel more love when engaged with these principles and practices: these "tame the dragon," transforming him into a young man.

Whenever I demonstrate an *aiki* approach to conflict and its resolution with a dragon, he is fascinated, asking excitedly, "How do you do that?!" and wants to learn. I'll begin with a typical he-grabs-my-wrist-I've-got-to-get-away-tug-of-war tussle, to show the common approach to conflict, pulling each other back and forth across the room. Next, I model the *aiki* response to the wrist grab by remaining calm and balanced, gliding gently forward and pivoting to his outside, lining up directly next to him, hip to hip with my arm extended along his arm. He naturally releases his grip. When I present the same demonstration to parents, they understand the difference immediately.

I re-read *The Hobbit*. In it, Thorin Oakenshield, the King of the Dwarves, says, "Dragons steal gold and jewels . . . wherever they can find them; and they guard their plunder . . . and never enjoy a brass ring of it . . . and they can't make a thing for themselves." In Western mythology, dragons steal and hoard gold and jewels. Dragon boys greedily grab attention and energy from their parents (and other grown-ups) in arguments, conversations, and conflicts. (That's why parents generally feel drained after dealing with their dragon-sons.) He "guards and hoards" the energy because he cannot use it creatively himself. He is afraid to develop his own power, and instead brings fear and destruction to other people. According to the famous mythologist Joseph Campbell, in Western mythology, slaying the dragon is symbolic for breaking free from fear to become more of the hero's true self: the liberation from what he does that holds him back from maturing. In Eastern mythology, Campbell describes dragons as symbols of vitality and bounty, representing the great and the glorious. The blending of these mythologies—liberation from greed and fear into bounty and vitality—is the path of *How Boys Become Men*.

Finally, I found that boys are fascinated with dragons, dragon tales and metaphors, which captivate their attention. They are drawn to stories of power, deeds, and transformation: all elements of "the hero's journey." Accessing this natural and developmental interest with symbols, stories, and tasks engages dragons in their own transformation.

Control and domination have been hallmarks of patriarchal power. As Hanna Rosin writes, that cultural model is kaput.[1] Yet parents, and many grown-ups, engage in control and domination activities with teenage boys in an effort to "get them to grow up." It will not work. Control and domination battles with their parents and other grown-ups depress boys' development. These battles create more conflict and acting out with adults, interfere with resolving their internal confusion, produce rage, frustration, and the loss of their potential contributions for the greater good. The boys cannot grow into men.

Humanity continues to evolve: a new concept of manhood is coming into being. I believe the boys are aching to develop into young men with purpose, passion, and power derived from developing internal self-confidence and expressed in accomplishment and service to humankind.

---

[1] "The End of Men," *Atlantic Monthly*, July/August 2010, Hanna Rosin.

Teenage boys live in the borderland between childhood and manhood. They are, despite common images, truly "men-in-the-making": full of potential but awaiting actualization. This borderland is full of promise and peril. Boys are waiting for "a new game in town." The old game, run by their boy mentality, traps parents and makes everyone miserable and prevents boys from becoming young men. It stops them from experiencing and engaging in the emerging cultural model of the mature masculine: where every boy develops into the man he was born to become.

Parents want their sons to succeed. To be happy. To fulfill their potential. *How Boys Become Men* is more than about behavior management. It offers a theoretically sound and practically tested set of knowledge and skills to mature boys into young men with purpose, passion, integrity, confidence, and compassion: the young men they were born to become. It guides parents and other adults to:

1. Understand the world of a teenage boy
2. Change their body conditions, their physical actions, and the manner and content of their speech, resulting in a radically different form of engagement
3. Establish positions of respect and authority creating more love and compassion
4. Be in charge of the flow of attention
5. Stop the incessant arguing, disagreeing, fighting, and battling for control
6. Stop being controlled and manipulated by their son
7. Practice modes of communication fostering his purpose, mission, and dreams
8. Create a context for him to develop authentic confidence, integrity, responsibility, and success

Give your attention to *How Boys Become Men* and put it into practice. It changes lives for parents and their sons. It brings boys into young manhood.

PART I

KNOWLEDGE OF THE BEAST

Knowledge of the Beast

Boredom's a pastime that one soon acquires . . .
—Elton John & Bernie Taupin

I'm bored. I worked all summer and earned good money. Back to school, it's the same old, same old.
—17-year-old boy

It's boring. There's nothing to do there.
—15-year-old boy

Teenage boys are bored.

Not possible? With all of the activities available to them and all of the entertainment opportunities and devices: X-box, Gameboy, Play Station, Wii, iPod, iPad, television, computer. Not to mention all the things they could do to help out around the house or to take care of their living environment (clean the bedroom): how can they be bored?

Activities lose their luster if they aren't fulfilling. They become "filling time." Entertainment does not satisfy the fundamental human need to engage in meaningful and purposeful activity. Neither does housework or cleaning the bedroom for a teenage boy (even though these are important).

Adults overlook something that is glaringly obvious to teenage boys. They are used to things being the way they are and they're ready for something different. From his perspective, he's not a little boy anymore. He's different. To him, everything else is pretty much the same. Despite common opinions, he is very ready for a change.

3

For example, boys are bored in school. From the moment they entered first grade, the routine has been the same. Sit at desks (or tables); read books, workbooks, worksheets; write assignments; answer questions; raise their hands to speak; take tests and quizzes. From age five or six right into adolescence, their bodies perform the same movements and their minds engage in the same type of activities. It doesn't matter that the course material changes or becomes more difficult. The environment and habit are no different. The boys are doing essentially the same things. They're bored with them and boredom breeds restless resentment and frustration.

Bert was a high school senior, a very bright guy who was well on his way to not graduating in June. From the outside looking in, it made no sense. He said:

> I worked hard all summer at a good paying job. I got myself up every day, worked long hours, never missed a day and earned a lot of money. In fact, I made as much as some teachers. I was really proud of myself. My confidence grew so much. I had done a man's job all summer and I felt like a man.

> Then I walked into school in the fall. It was the same old thing. I wasn't any different to them. The same stupid rules telling me what I could and couldn't do. Teachers and administrators treating me like a kid. The boredom set in immediately and I got angry. When they changed the requirements and added one more English class for graduation, I thought, screw it. I'm not doing this anymore.

As far as he was concerned, he'd grown up. He had demonstrated complete responsibility regarding his job and reaped the benefits both in money and in maturity. It was appalling to be in an environment that would not and could not allow him to function at his maturity level. School offered him nothing congruent with his development or any opportunity to continue developing as he had through the summer. "Same old, same old" equals boredom.

It starts much earlier than the senior year of high school. It's usually in full bloom in middle school. With all due respect to my colleagues in education, the process of school is too often incongruent with the development of a young man.

It's not really different with families. For better or worse, the dragon has lived with the same people all of his life. The habits, patterns, and relationships by and large have not changed very much. Regardless of divorces, blends, and other kinds of modifications, the boy knows enough about his family members, as well as their roles and modes of operation, that he feels as if there is nothing else to learn (which is not true) and no growth is taking place (true too much of the time). And it's no fun anymore. Frankly, he's bored with the whole thing.

Parents like to think they know their children. Perhaps. I'm certain the children know them. They've watched their parents since birth and have soaked in every habit, every nuance, every feeling quality, every aspect of their personalities. They especially know what sets them off: their "buttons"—and boys push them relentlessly.

Why? Partially because they are bored. In a sense there is nothing better to do, so why not get a rise out of Mom or Dad. It's a game and it's fun and it's predictable and they can win each and every time. If there were a better game in town, an opportunity that were more challenging and engaging to their growth and development, they'd go for it. But most of the time, there isn't, so it's one more time around the family Monopoly board—pass Go and collect $200.00.

For many parents, the whole game doesn't make sense. Mom is just trying to get her son to stop ragging on his little sister, or to clean up his room, or do his homework, or empty the dishwasher, or take out the garbage, or shut off the television and go to bed. Perfectly reasonable.

For the "dragon," the pattern, the way of relating is the same thing he's been used to for years, whether it's nagging, pleading, threatening, bargaining, or simply asking. Same program, different day. It's boring. For him, it's a parent-and-little boy routine that he knows all too well. Nothing new, so he lights Mom's or Dad's fuse and watches the fireworks.

Why in the world would they want to get all the negative attention: the yelling, arguing, and punishment? It's better than the alternative: unmitigated boredom.

Finally, boys are bored in their communities. Teenage boys complain constantly how boring it is where they live: there's "nothing to do." As far as they're concerned, everything is the same: same streets, same locations, same activities, same people all doing the same stuff. There is nothing new to spark their interest and pleasure. Dragons discard familiar activities and change friends. They don't find the community offering the kinds of challenges and opportunities necessary to grow and develop. So they're bored.

Adults hate being bored. Teenage boys are no different. What is different is they're not opposed to acting out their boredom. Boredom is very misunderstood. It is dangerous to the human spirit. Keeping busy to avoid being bored masks the symptom; no change in the cause.

Dragon boredom is amplified from a new awareness born with puberty: they're not entirely in the world of play anymore and the grownups are not infallible. It is magnified by the conditioning— there is enough entertainment and stimulation to keep them from being bored. Their imaginations and consciousness are stifled. The crowning touch is the virtual absence of socially validating endeavors that are developmental, meaningful and purposeful for developing into a young man.

Teenage boys are bored. It's not good.

Teenage boys are afraid.

This really surprises grown-ups. There is a certain irony to the bumper sticker on boys' cars and trucks: "no fear." Nothing could be further from the truth. Probably the greatest secret teenage boys keep is that they're scared. They don't act like it, but that is it: it's an act. Despite all the bravado, prancing and preening, cool postures, and reckless behavior, the fact is they are afraid. It just happens to be the last thing they're going to admit . . . and the most important thing they cover up.

Teenage boys will do everything they can to steer the grown-ups clear of the fact that they're scared. All the bluster, obnoxiousness, withdrawal, and claims to independence distract the adults from recognizing the boys are afraid. Unfortunately, too often the grown-ups believe the act, or at least don't know what else to do.

In the code of boyhood, being afraid is absolutely unacceptable. Boys learn this early in life and develop perfectly functional dramas to avoid it. "I don't care." "Whatever." "Doesn't matter." I've never met a boy who didn't deny being afraid, who didn't put on a show to attract attention away from being afraid. It's part of the old masculine model: men are fearless. Boys learn it early, and their play and life experiences practice the model.

John was a high school junior who had a very challenging go of it in school since first grade. A friendly fellow, he worked hard because he wanted to graduate. Still, he was drowning in his math class. He paid attention, did his homework and turned it in, but he was failing. He said, "I just have a hard time understanding some of this stuff." I said, "why don't you ask the teacher for help?" Perfectly reasonable question from an adult point of view. He looked at me, then dropped his eyes to the floor without a word. I nodded my head and said, "Afraid. I understand that." His head popped back up and he looked at me quizzically. I went on, "How many guys do you see strolling up to the teacher either during class or afterwards asking for help?" He answered, "None." I continued, "Ever?" and he said, "Never."

I put my hands up in the air and said, "Boys don't do that, do they? God forbid they show that they don't know or understand something. They'd look weak or stupid, or both." He smiled big time and said, "That's the truth." I went on, "So why should you be different from everyone else? Of course you're going to be afraid to look weak or stupid. Are you going to strut on up there confidently in front of everyone else and ask the teacher for help, right?" He laughed and said, "No way." I finished with, "Being afraid of feeling weak or looking stupid is stopping you from doing what is good for you. You want to live the rest of your life like that?"

Despite the changes in gender roles over the past thirty years, boys believe emotions are weak, and weak is bad. They should "take it like a man," not be a "sissy," or worse, a "girl," and have feelings. Except anger, of course, which "feels strong" despite of the fact that boys experience themselves as "out of control" or "trying to control" which makes them feel "weak" because they should be able to control themselves. Then they're ashamed for "having lost it" afterward when they're not busy blaming and justifying themselves. The fact is, they're afraid of their feelings.

Teenage boys are afraid because they don't have a clue as to who they are and where they stand. Their boy identity won't hold in the cutthroat competitive culture of teenage boys. Who they are in relation to their peers is as unstable as can be: even "good friends" can turn on them at the drop of a hat. There is a constant up and down in the teenage boy world. He may be popular one minute, not the next, in with one group of friends, then he doesn't belong. Friends are friends one day, but quite possibly not the next week.

Since teenage boys refuse to act afraid, they resort to all kinds of shenanigans, including acting absolutely obnoxious, super-cool, butt-kissing, and the cutup clown to fill a role. For many, it is fit in, at all costs. For others, it is find a quiet niche where no one will bother you. And there are always some who make their stand by not fitting in at all.

There are boys who recoil at the constant competition for nothing and take on a persona to keep people away. They adopt a social manner and/or dress pretty much guaranteed to ostracize themselves from the other kids. It is a painful form of self-protection: they are frightened to the point of self-imposed exclusion.

Teenage boys are afraid of girls. Generally, they are absolutely lost knowing who they are in relation to girls. Watching their show will mislead you. Whether they're first-rate flirts or way-behind wallflowers, their self-concept and self-image is fraught with fantasy and peril. They're plain scared.

A very bright and articulate thirteen-year-old had a reputation as a smart, geeky nerd. He was very comfortable with it. His position was secure in his opposition to the "popular" kids and identification with the other smart nerds. He exuded self-importance and confidence. One problem. Girls paid no attention to him. Being a geeky nerd gave him few chances to talk with them. When it came to girls, he was as awkward as a fish climbing a tree and, like most thirteen-year-old boys, he wanted a girlfriend. The boy was terrified.

Even the so-called cocky, self-assured studs are scared. They put on a great show-and-tell to try and score, really for the other boys, because the girls could care less. They are lost dogs either after they've "won," and/or in trying to relate in any personal, meaningful way.

Why should teenage boys be scared of girls? Because girls have feelings, because girls elicit feelings in the boys which they are embarrassed and confused about, because girls relate to and act on their feelings entirely differently than boys, and because girls are interested in relating and boys are interested in winning. They're lost and scared. So they do what boys do when they're scared: act cool, tough, nonchalant, withdrawn, and disinterested. It's an act. They're scared, especially with many teen girls currently being sexually provocative and aggressive.

Teenage boys are profoundly afraid of becoming men. It scares them silly. It looks boring, no fun, difficult, and depressing. They're afraid they don't have what it takes to be successful. They're afraid of what the future has in store for them and the rest of humanity. They're afraid: feeling alone, inadequate, and unprepared. They do not want to grow up and become men. This is not small potatoes: it is deep and significant.

Alan, a high school senior, said right after he turned eighteen, "I'm not interested in growing up. I'm going to play for as long as I can." Questioned about when he thought he would be ready, he answered, "Oh, maybe when I turn 26 or something. I don't really want to be a grown man. What fun is that going to be?"

Another eighteen-year-old boasted, "I should be able to do whatever I want. I'm eighteen and I should be able to make my own decisions, go wherever I want, whenever I want and not have to answer to anybody. Why should I have to listen to my father's rules?"

When he was asked, "Well, why don't you do that? You're eighteen. Why don't you just go live your life as you want?" He became very quiet, leaned forward in his chair and returning my look said quietly, "I'm scared. I don't know how I'd support myself. What am I going to do, work at McDonald's? How will I live? I'm used to having a really good life."

A thirteen-year-old once said, "I want to stop things at seventeen or eighteen, just before high school graduation. That would be perfect. I can drive, go wherever I want, be around my friends, but not have to be responsible for anything. Not have to work and support myself. That would suck."

It's not just that they don't like the image of being a man (which most of them don't); it's that they're afraid of it. They aren't confident they can do it; they're scared of the "responsibilities" and afraid of the "boredom." It's not limited to young men who may be challenged academically or struggling socially. It's pervasive, including the bright, talented, and socially active ones. And it will be the absolutely last thing they are going to show adults, especially their parents. They put on a fool's parade.

Unfortunately, the important grown-ups in their lives are too often fooled and drawn into the drama. Dragons are constantly demanding more freedom, determined to decide for themselves, and chastising parents and teachers for interfering and not understanding. They boast that grown-ups are unnecessarily restrictive, hopelessly out of touch with their reality, or just plain stupid. Their mouths and behavior claim, "If you'd only leave me alone and let me do what I want to do, everything will be fine."

Bruce was sixteen years old. He smoked a fair amount of marijuana, drank his share of beer, smoked cigarettes, and swore like a sailor.

After working together individually for a couple of months, he agreed to include his parents to resolve their conflicts. In a typically very heated session, Bruce ruthlessly berated his parents for their "ridiculous" curfew. Twelve-thirty on the weekends was outrageous when every other boy stayed out at least until 2:00 am, if not later. The onslaught of profanity and abusiveness was a regular event. Mom cried her eyes out and Dad chomped at the bit, rubbing his right fist in his left hand. Their reactions fueled his vehemence.

Matter-of-factly, I said, "If it is so bad, why don't you move out?" He bellowed, "Yeah, I'm gonna move out, you xz&#%$." I commented, "You come in here week after week and tell them what awful parents they are and how they're ruining your life. You're sixteen. Why don't you just take yourself up to the county seat, go to the clerk's office and file papers for emancipated minor status and get on with your life?" "Yeah," he shouted again. "I'm outta here. I'm gonna live with a friend and stop this . . ."

Dad looked up from across the room and said, "Oh, we can't do that. We have financial obligations." I looked back at him and said, "If he moves out, you won't have those financial obligations anymore." "OOHHHhh," he responded.

The boy sat up like he had a rocket in his rear-end. "Hey, wait a minute. What's going on here?"

"If it's so bad, why don't you move out?" was the answer. It got really quiet in the room.

Bruce was no more ready to move out than a fish is to fly. He was all bluster, show, bravado, and totally incapable of providing for himself and living a responsible adult life. Moving out was pure fantasy . . . and so was all of his strength. The only appearance of strength he had came from berating his parents.

Teenage boys are afraid of having more emotional power than their parents. It's a half-truth that they revel in being disrespectful and humiliating their parents. It's a game. One with very high stakes. It's one the grown-ups play unwittingly and, from the boy's point of view, lose with remarkable frequency to everyone's disadvantage.

Consider this common family scene: The boy has not met some family expectation or has done something wrong, and he defends, provokes, argues, rationalizes, calls them names, swears, or something else, OR acts nonchalant, like he doesn't care, it's no big deal, what are they upset about . . . whatever . . . and Mom or Dad just goes ballistic . . . he's "pushed their buttons."

Now, the parents, before they lose it, are simply asking their son to comply with what they consider are reasonable expectations and getting upset when he opposes them. For the boy, when they lose it, he thinks, "Ha! They aren't acting any more grown up than I am. They can't handle their feelings any better than I can. In fact, worse, because I can push them around. This is being an adult? This is it, the end of the maturity train? Great, so what have I got to look forward to? This isn't right. I don't like it. It scares me!"

Teenage boys need their parents.

Teenage boys will do everything they can to steer the grown-ups clear of the fact that they're scared. All the bluster, obnoxiousness, withdrawal, and claims to independence distract the adults from recognizing the boys are afraid. Parents tend to be shocked by the idea that their teenage sons need them. "Yeah, right," they remark. "He needs me to chauffeur him, feed him, clean his clothes, and buy him stuff. Other than that, I'm useless. He needs me about as much as I need a hole in my head!"

Dragons tell their parents to shut up, leave them alone, call them names, give single-syllable answers to questions, and live with their faces in their X-boxes, Play Stations, Nintendos, cell phones, computers, and televisions and their ears in their iPods. They hang with their friends, or in their rooms, and act like parents are absolutely the last people on Earth they want to be around.

Great routine. Well practiced and executed. It's a lie . . . pure theater . . . an act. Don't believe it.

The reality is, despite all appearances, teenage boys need their parents very much. All of their antics are dependent on the safety and security of the family: on the reliability and familiarity with their parents (and siblings). Without that security and familiarity, their ballooned egos go *thwwwwwp*.

Consider the story of the sixteen-year-old impaling his parents for their ridiculous curfew. The pattern of that story was that the boy would berate one or both of his parents. His mother would cry, beg, plead, and try to flee to get him to stop. The boy would predictably get worse. If Dad was home, he'd jump on his white stallion to rescue Mom from the boy's onslaught. Fists flew, CDs crashed, and Mom cried more. People stormed off to their rooms and "quiet" reigned until they passed Go, collected $200, and started again.

When Dad realized that my suggestion that his son move out meant real independence for all of them, the boy backed up as fast as he could. The fantasy of moving out fizzled immediately. He couldn't support himself financially or emotionally. He needed his parents.

Or consider the second story of the high school senior living with his father who complained he should be able to do whatever he wanted to because he is eighteen and old enough to make his own decisions. After he said he was scared to move out, he continued with "How am

I going to support myself? What am I going to do, work at McDonalds?" He was not ready to go: he still needed his parents.

A drastic example was a sixteen-year-old whose parents recently divorced. He lived with his mom and sister except for periodic visits with Dad. We worked out the kinks in the daily lives of him and Mom pretty quickly. But, his school grades were a roller coaster ride. It came out he was smoking marijuana regularly. Each time Mom confronted him, he backed off the weed and his grades went up.

The roller coaster always went down. The kid would start smoking again, sticking it to his parents, and his grades bottomed out. Mom was especially incensed because he smoked on the porch outside her home where the whole neighborhood could watch him, including the police if they drove by. She was afraid of a drug bust that could cost her her home. If the police raided the house thinking there was a drug dealer operating there, they could confiscate her home, car, and all of her belongings. Mom explained this to the boy each time she confronted him.

The boy was bright, especially with programming computers, which he loved to do. Dad had a car ready to give him and was considering backing the boy in a computer programming business if his grades stayed up. But, Dad refused to believe the boy was in and out of marijuana abuse and offered to pay the kid to keep his grades high.

After the third roller coaster ride, Dad woke up. He met with Mom and me, and they settled on a plan. They returned to her home that night, sat down with their son and presented him with a written document which read: *C's or better in school, after-school job, no drugs/ alcohol, random and unannounced drug tests, and chores done on time.* They told him to go upstairs with the document and think it over very carefully. When he was done thinking about it, to come down with either the paper signed or with his suitcase packed ready to leave right then and there. After thirty minutes, he came down with the paper signed. Bright as he was, he was not ready to be independent. The boy needed his parents. A lot.

There is little social support for the reality that teenage boys need their parents. Just the opposite. First of all, needing is "weakness" and they hate weakness, and therefore needing. So there is little chance they're going to say openly, "I need you," or what they need. They're going to do their best to cover it up and confuse their parents. They act like their parents are dorks: who needs them? They'll avoid or ignore them. Parents too often are mystified and throw up their hands in utter frustration.

Secondly, it's common for boys to ally with their friends against their parents. Supported by peer pressure and friends, the boys say, "I don't need you. I have my friends to talk to" and too often the parents cower and back down saying, "I tried, but what can I do?"

Rarely do teenage boys actually talk with their friends about subjects that are personal and important to them other than trouble and complaints about their parents, teachers, or other kids. Their friends are as ignorant as they are. What they may get is solace and a semblance of connection and belonging which is often not reliable. What they don't get is reality, a perspective and depth that has wisdom and future.

Thirdly—and very influential and powerful—the marketplace and media, our popular culture, promotes the illusion that teenage boys do not need their parents. They're depicted as smart, savvy, independent, in fact superior to adult men—a solid, independent market.

In popular culture, teenage boys are "cool," knowledgeable, and together. They're smarter than the grown-ups and they don't need anyone else, except their tribe. At the same time, the marketplace and media contrasts the "cool" teenager with the bumbling, foolish, easily duped, emotionally weak, immature grown-up.

The film *Ferris Bueller's Day Off*, marketed as a comedy, captures the image of the supposedly independent, albeit outlandish, young teenage male. He fools his parents and outsmarts the bumbling, oafish high school principal.

Popular culture idolizes and markets to youth. It portrays age as weakness, often ridiculing adulthood and maturity. When programming and advertising promote communication between teenage boys and grown-ups, it is to share buying products, talk about something current in teen culture, or to poke fun at adulthood. The conversation and message is steered back toward adolescence, not forward into adulthood.

Given all of this, no wonder it's close to impossible for parents to recognize that their sons need them. Unfortunately, when parents buy into the sham that their sons don't need them anymore, it's a fire sale. They end up with heartaches and aggravation. It's one fight after another over issues that never resolve because the premise is false and the issues are really red herrings.

In mythology and tales, dragons are dangerous and speak in riddles. Teenage boys are no different. They'll threaten you, tempt and test you, and burn you when you fall prey to their antics. Their needs are in code: the clues are in their language and in the patterns of their behavior. Parents and other adults are challenged to decipher the code.

Teenage boys need their parents. They need different qualities than what they needed when they were little boys. Teenage boys need mature modeling, boundaries, inspiration, encouragement, solace, strength, kindness, firmness, opportunities, practice, and safety. Most importantly, they need their parents not to believe they're not needed: to see through the performance to the real need, and not be controlled by their act.

Teenage boys are not ready to grow up. They're basically ignorant and scared about adult realities. They are not developing confidence in themselves nor a sense that they can handle the future. They need their parents to help make their way into young manhood. It is a necessary skill . . . it is also deeply satisfying.

Teenage boys crave real and meaningful challenge and responsibility.

This goes beyond making their beds, picking up their clothes, and taking out the garbage. There is nothing wrong with doing those activities. Those contributions to the household operation are important. They're members of the family, and giving and receiving are how a family functions.

However, real and meaningful challenge and responsibility emerge from their interests, and employ the talents, skills, and abilities that they've developed; what they experience then has value and a larger purpose. By the time a boy reaches adolescence, he has become competent in certain areas—he's learned some things, developed some skills, can accomplish tasks, has demonstrable abilities. Now he is ready, not only to use them, but to go beyond them.

Many parents have said, "Hah! He only wants to sit around, eat, and play video games, unless he's talking on the phone, downloading music, or on Facebook or texting his friends." Yes, that's true. Not only is that what everyone else is doing (so there is a social context), but what else is there for him to do? From his point of view, there's nothing else to do, and everything else he's used to: it's boring.

Very few teenage boys are offered an opportunity to exercise the skills and talents they've developed. Rarely can they employ their abilities and be recognized and valued by the larger social community. Generally, the opportunities they do have are either school or sports related. Often it remains a context that they are used to and still recognized as kids without a contributing social value to their communities.

Teenage boys are on the road to manhood, but are not getting much practice as "men-in-training." They're still viewed as kids, just bigger. This flies in the face of reality, a reality that they are well aware of. They're not kids anymore. They can do stuff, be useful, make a contribution. But, it just isn't happening. No choice but to just act like a big kid. A restless, edgy, chomping-at-the bit, big kid.

George was thirteen years old, not particularly attractive, and his habit was to annoy people. His school grades weren't good, he was frequently in trouble, and the kids picked on him for his poor looks and annoying behavior. To complete the picture, he was arrested for shoplifting and sentenced to probation. His community service was volunteering at a home for older folks. He said, "I'd much rather be at the home than at school. When I'm at the home, I feel important. I'm doing something that matters to people. I feel valuable. When I'm at school, I'm bored, picked on, and get into trouble."

As a thirteen-year-old volunteer, he didn't have the most glamorous job in the home. He delivered food, cleaned up messes, and emptied bedpans. To him, it was the difference between night and day. He used his skills and had a positive effect on the residents and employees at the nursing home. They valued his contributions, and so did he.

He could do those jobs and more. His social skills—warmth, friendliness, courteousness, respect—were qualities that were absent in the context of school, but at work were employed in a manner that benefitted everyone. The silver lining in a court conviction gave this young man a chance to show his stuff.

By the time puberty sets in, boys are emerging from the world of imaginative and imitative play. Now it's time to put the skills they've practiced throughout boyhood to use in a real way. They're ready to push the edge—not just test out their abilities, but to grow them, take them to the next level. Biologically, boys haven't changed that much. Less than a hundred years ago, they were making valuable contributions to society by the time they were teens. Developmentally, they are ready to move beyond child status.

Sam became a skilled scuba diver during a family vacation. He got good at it very quickly and devoted most of his free time to diving. His parents, and the adult instructors, recognized his proficiency and acknowledged it. Simply, his parents, especially his dad, went to him with questions and relied on him during dives. On one dive, his dad got into some serious trouble and Sam saved him.

"Real and meaningful" to boys, refers to a concrete sense from their subjective points of view. The activity must have a purpose and meaning to them and a value they see to the greater good for which they are recognized. Scuba diving was more than a sport; it was an activity that was dangerous, with life or death consequences. Through demonstrating his skills, Sam's status changed in his family. He was no longer just "their son." He now took his rightful place as a "young man" with something to contribute of comparable value to the grown-ups.

Teenage boys are ripe and ready to have a useful, valuable place in the world. They're hungry for contexts and experiences that usher them into the beginning stages of adulthood, where they demonstrate their abilities, receive appropriate recognition, and are elevated to a more developmentally realistic status.

When they don't get those opportunities, they are going to create them within the context of their peer culture. And the peer culture exists both symbiotically and in opposition to the adult culture. They develop ways that are against the grown-ups who "don't understand them" and "try to keep them in their place." Teenage boys fill that logical developmental need with boy versions of activities: versions that grown-ups will view as "testing" and "making bad choices" because the boys are challenging themselves by "trying to get away with" something. It's a lose-lose situation: the grown-ups either view it as "They're just being boys" (which they are, but they're supposed to be growing into men), or as proof of their immaturity and irresponsibility and lack of trustworthiness.

It is possible to tell the difference between an activity that is genuinely real and meaningful to dragons, and a version of "what can I get away with." The litmus test includes: 1) does his sense of self-esteem/self-confidence increase and 2) is he recognized for his value and contribution to society. When it is genuinely real and meaningful, the answer is unequivocally "yes" to both questions.

It is so obvious it is easily missed and taken for granted. Fourteen-year-old Alan decided during his freshman school year he wanted a summer job to earn some money. He landed one at a local restaurant as a dishwasher. After a couple of weeks working he said, "The job is great! I get the dishes washed, I'm meeting different people and learning about their lives. The managers like my work and tell me and I get paid to boot. It's great."

His confidence grew because he demonstrated new competence, in a new environment, was valued for his contribution and received recognition and he earned money too.

When the activity is not real and meaningful to teenage boys, the answer is "no" to both questions. When it is a "bigger kid" version of "what can I get away with," then he gets a temporary inflation of his ego, his sense of "I'm powerful, you're not" and he'll get peer recognition. The shadow side of this is getting caught. Instead of an increase in self-esteem and real confidence, he gets a substantial decrease in self-esteem, decrease in confidence and his recognition from the grown-up world is negative twice over. Firstly, he screwed up by making "bad choices," and secondly he demonstrated his "immaturity" and lack of "responsibility" instead of the opposite. This is bad news for the boy, his parents, and the community.

Jordan was a high school junior with a double life. He worked hard in school, earned very good grades, and was a successful athlete. It had been his practice since elementary school. Midway through 11th grade, he started racing cars down the local highway at speeds in excess of 100 miles per hour and stealing from stores with a friend. He didn't need the stuff. He got caught. His parents went through the roof. He's embarrassed, ashamed, full of ridiculous excuses, and humiliated. It turned out Jordan was chomping at the bit to explore new areas, especially auto mechanics, and establish himself as a young man.

The electronic world offers a fantasy version of the real McCoy. Boys get to pretend they are competent, effective, talented, meaningful, and purposeful in a whole slew of games, either on-line, computer-based, or on video systems. They genuinely develop a high level of skill playing games, and like boyhood fantasies, have the freedom to choose either a heroic role or an evil role. The game could care less. They are even free to "cheat," hunting down codes on websites to "win" easier: a video version of "what can I get away with." The attraction is powerful: boys of all ages experience a sense of power and effectiveness in a fantasy world. Zero growth in the real world.

Parents are often perplexed, if not shocked, when a teenage boy suddenly stops all the activities he's enjoyed: sports, Boy Scouts, school and church clubs, anything and everything. It doesn't make sense and they wonder what is going on with him. Talking with him usually gets no results: "I dunno. I just don't want to do it anymore." The fellow is ready to make a mark, conquer new territories, use his skills in the real world, and be recognized for his abilities. He looks to the Real World, the world of grown-ups to provide challenges and opportunities to pull him further along the road toward manhood.

Teenage boys respond to reality. If it isn't real and meaningful to them, they're going to ignore it. If what they are faced with—if their actions in the world in relationship to other people do not further their growth and development—doesn't draw out their need to put into practice the skills and abilities they've developed and pull them past their comfort zones into more of themselves as young men, they're going to either blow it, retreat into their own best attempts to move into manhood, or recede into a make-believe world.

This encompasses way too much of their lives. It includes most, if not all, of school, most of their family lives, and a large portion of their social lives with friends and peers. In the absence of "real and meaningful," they feel life is a make-believe reality and they respond to it in make-believe ways: fantasy, video and computer games. They create alternate realities in an effort to establish meaningfulness. They're acts of defiance and rebellion, but not simply in the common interpretation. They are rejecting, with all the brilliance of their inventive, creative, desperately frightened energy, the image of the grown-up world. The same is often true for a boy seemingly following the "correct" path but going nowhere.

Cal was an eighteen-year-old who "left" college to return home. The school wasn't eager for him to return because his grades reflected more time drinking beer and partying than studying. Surly and reluctant to talk, his parents were furious after his second arrest for minor in possession of alcohol.

He was in hot water. Mom and Dad weighed in heavily about his lack of responsibility, poor judgment, bad attitude, and over-indulgence in beer. The judicial system had him hanging in limbo. He and the two other boys had fled the scene. Although he had voluntarily turned himself in, he was scared. He acted as if he were prepared to fight, but his world was collapsing around him.

"What happened?" I asked him once we were alone.

"I was out cruisin' with a couple of other guys and havin' a few beers when the police spotted us. We pulled off onto a two-track, jumped out of the car and scattered out of there on foot. I knew I couldn't get caught again and I just didn't think. I was scared to death so I ran as fast as I could. The cops tried to catch us on foot, but they weren't in shape to do it. I ran like a deer on the fly."

"So then what happened?"

"I couldn't go back to the car so I started walking. I walked all the way home."

"Then what?"

"I told my parents and we went right down to the police station so I could turn myself in. It was the right thing to do and I knew I had to do it. Now I don't know what'll happen. I'm terrified I'll lose my driver's license and the chance to get my truck."

"What do you mean?" I asked.

"I came home from college with one goal in mind: to work so I can save money to buy a bad-ass truck. I've had hand-me-down cars since I got my driver's license. I've got it all picked out. All I want is that truck."

There was a lot standing between him and getting his truck. First was a long history of conflict in his family in which he had a significant role. Second was his drinking. Third was his status with the law. Fourth was he didn't have a job. If he were ever going to get that truck, he'd have to face all four areas: he'd have to move from acting like a boy to beginning to be a man.

He wanted that truck. He quit drinking, got two jobs, confronted his role in the family and began building trust with his parents, and followed the terms of his probation to the letter. Several months later, with his parents' help, he made a down payment and drove off with his "bad-ass" truck.

Going to college and beer-partying all of the time was not real and meaningful to him. Something else made him tick. Craving that truck and following his desire to work and earn money contained the seeds of his soul unfolding into the future. It opened up previously invisible doors of opportunities to practice and learn more work skills that he truly enjoyed. He received grateful recognition for the important contributions he made to his employers. His self-confidence grew by leaps and bounds; he held a trusted position in his family, and he became a man in the eyes of the community. When he went before the judge at the end of probation, the young man had the courage to ask for permission to tell the court his whole story. The judge was so impressed, she invited him to join her for lunch.

When the adult world doesn't come through, the need is met through the dark side. The boys create activities with real dangers and risks which they intend to pull off outside of an adult view. The developmental downside is no growth for the boy. Regardless of the risks, he is playing the same game he's played for years. It's just a more "sophisticated" version of the boy game "what can I get away with."

No growth for the boy is unbearable. Teenage boys crave challenge and responsibility that is real and meaningful to them. They are poised forward, on the threshold of what we use to call "coming-of-age" experiences. They cannot create it alone: it requires the adult world's full participation.

Teenage boys are agents of change.

Despite all appearances, they are trying to bring change into every area of their lives.

Parents say, "Right! Cannot be. Then why does he keep doing the same stupid things? He knows what's going to happen. Breaks curfew . . . this is what is going to happen. Takes the car when he's not supposed to . . . this is what is going to happen . . . doesn't do his school work or turn in his homework or his grades are poor . . . this is what is going to happen . . . why does he keep doing it over and over again? It defies rational logic."

Well, it would defy rational logic if the parents and the boy had the same premise. They don't. They are operating from very different principles and dynamics.

Teenage boys are masters of disguise, masters of deception, and masters at game playing. When they're playing a game (which is almost always) and they draw the grown-ups into it (which is most of the time), it's both fun for them and it's very frightening. Very frightening! Why? Because the change they're trying to invoke, which they don't even understand consciously most of the time, does not happen. And that scares them. A lot.

Truthfully, teenage boys are agents of change. They are seeking the next edge, the next level of development. They feel, in their bodies, the sense of absolutely having to grow. Do they recognize this sense? Most of the time, no. Will they talk with their parents about it? Not likely. Instead, they provoke situations to start something going, to get a row started because, one, it has a pay off in the game and two, in their inept way, they're trying to provoke a change.

Characteristic of boys, their way of doing it falls flat on its face. He's just a boy. He does not know how to promote a change effectively. He's young, inexperienced, and unskilled at change making. Even though he is slowly waking up to his role as an agent of change, he is not yet the leader or effector because he does not have the power to pull it off. That power belongs to the grown-ups. So his change-making happens in a boy way: sloppy, messy, ineffective, and more often than not misunderstood.

It is misunderstood because, they're communicating, through their behavior, in code. It is a code like any encryption, with distraction and deception. Generally, grown-ups miss the code, fall for distraction and get embroiled in the game. Once the game commences, it's curtains for the change this round. Done . . . finished. The boys rule.

The boys seek change by provoking struggles with grown-ups. The conflict is the signal that they need a change. Now the misbehavior, breaking curfew, taking the car, poor school performance, can take on an entirely new light. The challenge is recognizing the signal, avoiding the entanglement, and engaging them in a manner that promotes real change. It is a tricky minefield because the parents want a change too and it is all too easy to become entangled in a misguided and misleading win/lose game. When the parents and other grown-ups decipher and understand the code, they're poised to respond to them actively and effectively to move the change along.

A second way teenage boys show they're agents of change is by defining themselves by what they are not: I'm not a jock . . . not a geek . . . not a goth . . . not my parents . . . not my brother or sister. He's effecting a change by not being like something/someone else. It's a negative way of identifying himself and of "belonging." It's built on a sand foundation because he does not have a clue to who he really is (and early on in adolescence, he's not supposed to). This is his starting point, the best change he can do right out of the gate. It's not the end point. Being "against" doesn't establish what he is "for" or "who he is" and won't automatically get him there.

A teenage boy is not going to walk up and say, "Hey, I'm feeling like it's time for me to figure out who I am." He'll act it out in all kinds of confrontation and/or withdrawal behavior with parents and other grown-ups. He'll point out how he's different from you, other family members, other boys, other people who don't "understand" him. It's all part of him being an agent of change, a code that something new and different is necessary from the adult world for him to develop.

A third aspect of being an agent of change is a teenage boy's efforts to develop what is uniquely him: his "genius." This notion usually sends grown-ups over the edge: "I don't see him doing anything," and "He's not that bright."

Genius, not in its usual context of extraordinary intelligence, but in the classic sense of his unique soul qualities, his unique purpose to be expressed and given to the world through his skills, talents, and abilities.

Grown-ups usually focus their attention, and try to focus the boy's attention, on "What are you going to be when you grow up?" or "What do you want to do?" Seemingly pragmatic, it is a pittance compared to the driving force of his "genius."

Early on in adolescence, something begins stirring inside of him, something generally below the surface, of wanting to do something, be something that is almost impossible to put into words. It propels him forward. It's a Truth about himself. Usually, grown-ups not only don't pay attention to it, they don't even look for it or think it's there, or misunderstand it, or judge it incorrectly. It may show as an interest, a kind of passion.

The boy will often try, in some often very awkward way, to express and develop it. Often, he'll keep it hidden. Frequently, he gives up before it can germinate. There is a lot that affects his "genius" and it is generally fragile.

It is a critical aspect of a teenage boy's growth. He's propelled forward into the world of manhood where his purpose and meaning are primary driving forces of his Life. His "genius," this soul quality, calls for attention at its very inception, its very first appearance at the onset of adolescence. It is a change he absolutely needs, and it is usually sorely missed.

Finally, teenage boys are agents of change by putting pressure on the family, by being a pain in the behind: irascible and cunning and clever and annoying and withdrawn and everything else imaginable. He's awakened to all of the ins and outs of his family, and senses where changes are important.

However, he's virtually useless at effecting the changes or even addressing the changes effectively because he does not have the power to pull it off. He doesn't have the power to be more mature than he actually is, so it comes out in game behavior. It is a paradox: he senses the need and importance of changes, pushes for them, but in a boy manner that is guaranteed to produce more of the same family quality that he's pushing against. He brings out "the worst" through his efforts, giving him more of what he knows should change.

The parents join right in. They end up with more of the same from him, and around and around it goes. This is "stirring the pot." There is no power, no change. But the truth is, change is exactly what the boy is seeking.

Grown-ups tend to focus on concrete practical changes: get the chores done, homework finished and turned in: changes in behavior. They think these are signs of "maturity" and "responsibility."

What is the change he is seeking? He seeks a developmental and dynamic change; a change that demonstrates a greater capacity of personal power, effectiveness, engagement in life. For teenage boys, everything is about power. And power is gravely misunderstood by both teens and grown-ups. He is seeking to bring into being the change he is developmentally designed for: to become a young man.

This change is not automatic. It requires initiation: a departure from the norm, real challenges and tests, discipline and training from the already-initiated, and a successful return where he is welcomed and recognized and treated as a young man instead of a boy.

The common approach is backwards. Teenage boys receive "freedom" because they are "old" enough or "all the other boys can" or the market and popular culture convince grown-ups he should have such and such object or freedom.

He will demand more freedom to make his own choices. If the freedom is granted without demonstrating the capacity to handle the power that comes with the freedom, he does not develop into a young man and continues to "act out" because the real change has not happened. More games; more conflict.

Teenage boys are agents of change.

Teenage boys are boys: everything is a game.

This really confuses grown-ups, especially when the boys are being a big pain. They're thinking, "What's the game with him being _____?"—fill in the blank for his behavior.

To get a grasp on "everything is a game," it's necessary to take a look at boys before they're teens. For little boys, everything is about play and strength. They are constantly playing at something: they play with each other, they play by themselves, and they play in relationship with other people, including grown-ups . . . play . . . play . . . play.

As boys, the fun is in the play: playing the game. They want to win. They really do not want to lose. But when they do, they tend to move on because the game is always re-starting. Two favorite games are "getting my way" and "what can I get away with."

It's not a game for parents. They are trying to accomplish a task, like get him dressed and off to school, or get his clothes or toys picked up and put away or his homework done or him get ready for bed. Their world-view is "getting him to do" something.

The world-view of a boy is entirely different. Getting the task done is not on his radar screen. He does not live in a world of "tasks." He's playing whatever he's playing and his playing is a part of everything he is doing. If he's "getting something done" he's at the very least imaginally playing through it. For boys, all of their games are about strength and power. They are about who's strong and who isn't, who's winning and who's losing, who's in control of what's going on and who's not and who's getting what he wants and who's not.

Boys play. Through play they learn the fundamentals of strength, power, and of human interactions and relationships. It's a game for them because they are boys.

Once a boy has entered teenage-dom, he's learned everything there is to learn from the "who's strong . . . who's not" game and all of the family interactions that revolve around it. He's got it down and virtually every interaction with someone in the family, especially his parents, is an expression of the game. In the game he gets the reaction he expects, the attention he expects, the outcome he expects. It's all a game and, as far as he's concerned, he's in charge of the rules.

When a game goes as expected, and the outcome is predicted, three things are going to happen. He's going to get bored, he's going to try and change it (and fail), and he's going to do it again and again. Even though he's older, with the potential to outgrow playing "win/lose" games, it won't happen without the right knowledge and skillful engagement. In its absence, the invisible element of "winning and losing" infiltrates everything he does.

He starts exercising his game skills to upset the apple cart, to challenge the "rule of law" and the "order of power" and exploit the weaknesses in the other players. He does it so masterfully that the grown-ups are usually either brought to their knees in frustration, or to a state of explosive chaos experiencing a loss of control that drives them nuts.

And they just cannot figure out, "Why does he do _____ ?" Fill in the blank.

Over the past few decades, because of professional psychological theories and practices that were popular for a time, the word "game" has taken on a very negative meaning. Phrases like "He's playing a game" or "He's being gamey" imply a deliberate intent to cause the outcome. It is devoid of a sense of play and implies malice. Grown-ups may be quick to tag teenage boys with malicious intent, as in "He likes to push my buttons" and "Why does he do that to me?" He is playing a game, but his intent is not to do harm: it's to win and/or provoke a necessary change.

"Game" in its simple sense involves play, rules, a time frame (be-ginning/middle/end), and an outcome—like a board game, sports game, or even a video game. The only difference is the players in his game may not be aware of the rules and have different ideas about the intended outcome. In fact, the boy is generally unaware of game! His intention is not consciously deliberate: he's just being himself on automatic pilot without thought.

Dragons are teenage boys and boys play games. At this point, he's the master of the game.

Teenage boys love to push buttons.

There are buttons on their computers, smart phones, iPods, iPads, Gameboys, Playstations, Wiis, X-boxes, remotes and on and on. Give him something he can program and has buttons to push (espe-cially with a screen) and he's halfway to heaven. He'll spend almost his entire waking life playing with the buttons.

Imagine a roomful of parents coming to listen to someone talk about teenage boys. The speaker walks in with a BIG box of buttons and passes a bunch out to each grown-up. Why? The buttons teenage boys love more than any others are the ones they "push" on the grown-ups, as in "he pushes my buttons." Perhaps his favorite activ-ity with parents is pushing their buttons.

In his eyes, parents and grown-ups come with all kinds of sensitivities, issues, pet peeves, and even important values that they get worked up about. He sees buttons in front of him in a dazzling array of lights and colors just aching to be pushed.

They're irresistible. So he pushes one or two and then, Wow . . . watch the incredible display of fireworks in three-dimensional color and sound, complete with actions and movements that initially captivate his attention but in time become boring.

But, he cannot resist those buttons. When they're there staring him straight in the face, he feels as if they're begging to be pushed. He's just got to . . . lean right in and . . . push those babies.

POW! There goes the show again! It is truly amazing. He'll either sit back and enjoy the performance or just jump right in and join the fun himself. It's like a family version of one of those mystery dinner/theatre performances where the audience gets involved with the characters in the story. Only, he's always part of the story in this one.

Parents ask, "Why does he do that? Why does he push my buttons?" This leads to all kinds of stress and strain. They start wondering whether there is something wrong with their parenting. Or they form all kinds of nasty and ugly opinions about their boys, which they usually feel guilty about too. And they talk about it with their friends and family and even with the boy, all to no avail. It happens over and over again, driving the grown-ups absolutely nuts! Try as they might, they just cannot seem to get him to quit pushing their buttons. He might take a break for a little while. A few days here and there. Maybe even a week or two. Then, he just cannot resist it any longer and . . . POW!, he DOES IT AGAIN . . . the little monster.

The really simple answer to the question, "Why does he push my buttons?" is because they're there, and teenage boys love pushing buttons.

Teenage boys will avoid losing at all costs.

To boys, everything is a "win/lose" game and they will avoid losing at all costs: period. This totally confounds parents and other grown-ups. Their boy is told to turn off the TV or get off the computer and come to dinner. Does he come to dinner? Absolutely not. Pick up his clothes from his bedroom floor? Doesn't happen. Get the garbage cans from the curb? There they remain in all of their glory.

What happens next? He loses privileges or gets grounded or has his cell phone taken away and can't take the car. He gets some other punishment or consequence intended to teach him a lesson and correct his behavior. He blows a gasket and expresses his feelings about the punishment and the parents in no uncertain terms. He skulks off to his room or storms out of the house or some other action certain to leave the situation messier and uglier than before.

Or he goes into silent mode and stares at you with an absolutely blank look on his face. Maybe it's more with a look like, "Boy, you are strange." Maybe he issues a "whatever" out of his mouth before he turns back to whatever he was doing before you "interrupted" him—or he just walks off.

"Why does he do this?" parents ask. They say, "I don't get it. If he would just do what I tell him to do, he'd have everything."

The same thing happens with "trying to get him to _____"—fill in the blank, as in trying to get him turn in his homework or put his clothes away or empty the dishwasher. None of them happen. The result is he does not have everything and the parents say, "I just don't get it."

Of course, how could the grown-ups "get it?" There is nothing wrong with their expectations. What could possibly be wrong with a teenage boy bringing up the garbage cans once a week, a task taking a few minutes max. What's the harshness in expecting him to emptying the dishwasher, another strenuous job requiring five minutes of effort. Parents think, "Just get with the program, Jack. What's so difficult?"

Look at the trade-off. Five minutes here bringing up the garbage cans, five minutes there emptying the dishwasher. Putting his clothes away, another five minutes. Joining the family for dinner, maybe 15 to 20 minutes. Grand total of 30 to maybe 45 minutes of "effort."

In exchange, he gets a cell phone, all of the household amenities (television with cable or satellite), high speed Internet (all of the social networks), a computer (or two or three), video game console (X-box, Playstation, Wii), iPod, iPad, and if he has a driver's license, access to a car.

Not a bad deal.

So, why doesn't he just do it, parents ask.

It's simple. If he does, they win. He loses.

He's a boy. Boys play games. Boy games are all win/lose operations. That's his world view. From that view, his parents are "trying to get him" to bring up the garbage cans, empty the dishwasher, do his homework, put his clothes away, and come to the table for dinner just like when he was a younger boy.

That's not going to happen. He's a teenage boy. Teenage boys will avoid losing at all costs . . . period.

PART II

POWER, CONFLICT, AND LOVE

POWER, CONFLICT, AND LOVE

Teenage boys are trying to grow into young men. At first glance, this may seem nuts. It is not. It is plain, simple fact. Once it is accepted and absorbed everything begins to change. The deeper it is accepted, the more it guides parents' understanding, the easier life is with their teenage son.

Grown-ups generally view teenage boys as problems. Certainly their behavior can be a huge problem. It just happens to be that their "problem activities" are a "symptom," a ruse, a distraction, a symbolic representation of something greater, deeper, more fundamental and important. That deeper meaning: teenage boys are trying to grow into young men.

When trouble occurs between a dragon and a parent, especially when he "starts" it, there is one action happening with different levels of meaning and purpose. The surface level—and the most obvious—is that he's trying to get the grown-up. He's playing a game, pushing his/her "buttons," he wants to win, and will avoid losing at all costs. It's a tried-and-true pattern, and he knows it.

When the parent argues, engages in a fight, or even has a "conversation" about his behavior, the boy is going to win and the parent is going to lose: there will be no change.

There is no change because below the surface level is a boy trying to grow into a young man and he needs your help to do it. The deeper meaning of his behavior is that he needs a change and the "below" level is more powerful than the "surface." He is developmentally ready to move into young manhood and he requires the necessary conditions, interactions, and relationships with his parents to pull it off. Arguing, fighting, and talking with him about his behavior isn't the help he needs. The dynamics of activity between the parent and him need to be different from when he was a boy or his boy games are going to continue to work and he will not mature. Everything related to power, conflict, and love must change, must develop to the next level to help the boy to become a young man.

Two axioms: for a teenage boy, everything is about power. For him to become a young man, he must develop his power beyond a boy level. The second axiom is the beliefs, ideas, and definitions for power, conflict, and love form actions by the boy and the parents that result in misery, arguing, frustration, and no maturing. There lies the analysis and the hope.

As far as the boy is concerned, parents have all of the power. Why? Because they control all of the things he uses, and they can punish him. He cannot punish them. Generally, parents feel like he has all of the power. Why? Because he can drive them crazy, because they cannot get him to do what they want, because he won't listen to them.

The conflict is similar: parents and boys are both trying to win by getting the other to change, to get someone to do something. The boys want to get their point across, get the parents to admit they're wrong, to get their way. The parents want him to obey, to do what they want him to do.

This is the form of love: mutual battles between the dragon and his parents.

In the conventional model (which is truly an early developmental phase), power is believed to be the ability to control—to dominate a person, place and/or event. It is measured subjectively: I have it; he does not. In game theory, it is a zero-sum game. This is what we believe. This is how we think. This is how we act and this is what is real. To exercise power is to exercise control and domination.

The conventional model of conflict is a contest with a winner and a loser. Webster's Online Dictionary states:

> 1 : fight, battle, war <an armed conflict>
> 2 a : competitive or opposing action of incompatibles : antagonistic state or action (as of divergent ideas, interests, or persons) b : mental struggle resulting from incompatible or opposing needs, drives, wishes, or external or internal demands
> 3 : the opposition of persons or forces that gives rise to the dramatic action in a drama or fiction

When there is a "conflict," each person wants to win and the other to lose. They cannot both win in this model. How does the loser feel? Bad. What is the loser going to do? Get back, get even, get revenge. This is what we believe. This is how we think. This is how we act and this is what is real. Conflict is a contest with winners and losers.

The conventional model of love is a strong affection for another.

Webster's Online Dictionary states:

> 1 a (1) : strong affection for another arising out of kinship or personal ties <maternal love for a child>

People show affection through caring, kindness, compassion: trying to be good and nice. But, in the face of power and conflict, this "love" goes right out the window and people are transformed into monsters. The boys are "dragons" and parents, in trying to "slay them" become "evil monsters," "ugly selves" who feel no love towards the boy whatsoever. When their buttons get pushed, parents light right up.

And they're angry at the boys for "pushing their buttons" and angry at themselves for blowing up. Parents feel guilty because they "should be able to do it better" or self-righteous and justified in "not letting him get away with it." This is what we believe. This is how we think. This is how we act. This is what is real. Love is the sense of strong affection.

Teenage boys are trying to grow into young men. It is a developmental process that they are biologically ready for. Dragons are ready for deeper, richer definitions and beliefs about power, conflict, and love: beliefs that build on the foundations they learned as boys and move them to the next level of maturity, into actions that are purposeful, meaningful, effective, and responsible, with honor and integrity. They are ready for the adult world to present it to them so they can interact with it and develop into it themselves.

Dragons are ready to understand that power is the embodied sense/experience of their own authority and the ability to act from it. This is commonly called "confidence" and/or "identity." It has no basis in control over another human being. Its basis is in personal authority and managing/directing one's actions.

Conflict is when two or more forces converge, creating the opportunity for something new and different to occur. This is the "hidden" creative potential in conflict: the potential for development and growth to occur. The opportunity is engaged by how people exercise power.

Love is the deeper, inclusive affection and care for all parties involved. It includes the deeper care to meet his need for development through demonstrating one's own maturity and integrity: to not be fooled by his games, to not be seduced or drawn into his games, to not be reduced to "childish" behavior oneself.

Absorbing these definitions/beliefs, integrating them into one's being so that actions emerge from an embodied sense of authority, an understanding that conflict is an opportunity to create change, and a felt sense of love for the boy and oneself, will revolutionize life with a teenage son.

The conventional views of power, conflict, and love produce "tug-of-war" scenarios with teenage boys. In the pictures below you can see how the reaction to being grabbed on the wrist results in a tug- of-war back and forth pulling between the parent and the teen. You can insert any number of words to this scenario. One common example:

"I need you to pick up your clothes."
"I'll do it in a minute."
"You said that the last time I asked you."
"I said I'd do it. Why're you always nagging me?"
"I'm not nagging you. I'm asking you to pick up your clothes and you don't do it."
"I said I'd do it. Just leave me alone already."
"If I leave you alone, you never get anything done."

Etc ... etc ... etc ...

Figure 1

The reverse is equally true. In these pictures, the boy is grabbing the parent's wrist. The words might go like this:

"I need you to take me to Joey's house."
"Not when you talk to me in that tone of voice."
"What tone of voice? Just take me to Joey's 'cause we're going out."
"I'm not going to be treated disrespectfully."
"I'm not being disrespectful. You're just annoying."
"Did you take the garbage out yet?"
"I said I'd do it. I'll do it when I get back from Joey's house."
"I'm not taking you now."
"Why not! I gotta go, c'mon, take me to Joey's."

Etc . . . etc . . . etc . . .

Figure 2

These are common scenarios. They happen daily between parents and boys. It doesn't matter "who starts it." It's a win/lose game because they're both trying to win and it goes on indefinitely. Battles won or lost: the "war" continues. The truth is, the parent loses the instant it begins!

To get a real feel for the action in the pictures, get a safe partner and act out each of these scenarios. Grab the partner's wrist. The partner will pull back. Now pull back in response. Back and forth to sense what happens in the body and mind. It isn't necessary to speak the words to feel what really happens. And what happens with an adult also happens with a teenage boy except the meaning of the experience is different for him.

It's similar because they both want to win. It's similar because they're both frustrated, upset, and/or angry. It's similar because they both feel like the other one has all the power. Parents get caught up in a win/lose game that their teenage son has known and understood since he was a little boy. It's in the form of "let's fight" or "let's argue." What's different for the boys, is the game is both fun and scary. Fun because they're used to it, and they win—while parents lose. Scary because the grown-ups don't behave any more maturely than the boys are behaving. Boys say: "They're not acting any more mature than me." They will keep playing it until the parents stop and set up a different game.

Grown-ups do not understand that as far as the boy is concerned, they've lost the instant some kind of "force," some kind of emotional reaction to "get him to do something," is used. What they lose is their own confidence, their own center of gravity, or their own relaxed and calm embodied sense of self. It's been given over to the dragon in the reaction. The parent's body posture displays the loss of a relaxed, calm, confident, center of gravity.

Figure 3

The boy wins because the parents behaved exactly as he knew they would. He got the response he expected. He got them.

What is invisible in this game is the mind. When the teen "grabs a wrist," the parent's awareness and attention focuses on the boy's actions. They become caught up in his agenda in reaction to his behavior. It's like "Oh my God, he's _____ ," their buttons are pushed, and their mind is locked on him. He's got them.

How does a boy know so easily he's got the parent? Boys live in their bodies, are very sensitive to physical space and acutely aware of touch, and have observed their parents for their whole lives. It takes almost nothing for him to know what is going on within his parent. He's so sensitive that, if he were holding a wrist and all a parent did was close the hand, no pull, no tug, simply close the hand, the boy would tighten his grip. He'd sense that reactive response and lock down. It's very subtle. The sense of "resistance" to his "force" results in two things: more force, and, he's won.

By the time a boy reaches puberty, no later than 14, he's ready for something new and different to happen. This win/lose game is old hat. Completely familiar. Nothing new to learn from it. He'll keep playing it as long as it's the only game in town. He's ready for a game that challenges him to grow and develop into a young man.

The same wrist grab is illustrated in the pictures below. What happens is totally different from the first sets of pictures. The parent is relaxed, comfortable, and open-hearted with an obvious "center of gravity," moving comfortably to the boy's side, turning and extending gracefully facing in the same direction. He lets go.

Figure 4

There is a complete absence of force. The parent does not lose confidence, does not lose a center of gravity, does not lose a relaxed and calm embodied sense of self. His/her attention does not become entangled with the boy's actions. She/he focuses on herself, her own well-being from which she moves and extends herself to align with her son. There is no "tug of war" because there is no resistance. From a relaxed, comfortable, confident, "center of gravity"condition, she/he can, without resistance, act effectively. The boy can learn how to develop into a young man in response to her model. Give up the old game: now there is a better game in town.

Will he do it immediately, the very first time? No. It requires practice, patience, and persistence on the part of the parents. But the truth is, boys are amazed by this exercise, and each one asks, "How do you do that?" He wants to find out how he can do it. He's ready to move along the developmental path into young manhood: to play "win/win." For him to develop his potential, it requires interactions with real adults that model and pattern the practice. He needs to be engaged in a reality where power is the embodied sense of authority and the ability to act from it, where conflict is the convergence of forces creating the possibility for change, and where love is maintained as an affection for all the parties involved and demonstrated by meeting his need for engagement in adult behavior.

There is nothing really mysterious or magical about it. Adults immediately understand this demonstration too! They're ready for something different. How they "see it" is everything. What the beliefs are really, deeply matters. It requires accepting the fact that teenage boys are trying to develop into young men, that they need grown-ups to engage with them in actions that model and demonstrate how to behave as an adult, and they are using the vehicle of conflict to make this need known.

Teenage boys only know how to play win/lose games. They're ready to move on to a deeper, truer, more mature experience of power, conflict, and love: one way beyond win/lose. They cannot do it by themselves. It requires interaction with real adults for context, modeling, and experience to develop. They are asking parents for help. This is love. Providing the help is also love.

Part III

Putting Power, Conflict, and Love into Practice

PUTTING, POWER, CONFLICT, AND LOVE INTO PRACTICE

Teenage boys are out to get their parents: to push their buttons and draw them into win/lose games. They "win" simply by parents joining in, because they're now operating at a child level. Bingo: game over. Although the boys will piss and moan that the parents always win because they have all the power and can punish them, it's dragon poop. Dragons know they've won and will do it over and over again.

The challenge for parents, and all the grown-ups facing teenage boys, is what to do when boys are out to push their buttons, when they're being dragons. How do they put the dynamics of power, conflict, and love into practice?

To be successful with teenage boys requires claiming your space, setting your rules of engagement, and acting. If the buttons are "lighting up"—the parent is losing it and going reactive—then create distance from the boy to claim your space, set your rules of engagement, and act. It is necessary to manage the space inside of you, outside of you, and your physical actions; speaking in a calm, normal voice tone and volume; and delivering your message where you are the subject.

The boy is in the kitchen yelling, swearing, calling his mother all kinds of profane names. Mom's elevator buttons are beginning to light up. She creates distance by leaving the room and going into the family room. She claims her space by sitting on a chair by an end table. She sets her rules of engagement. When her son follows her into the family room smoldering and swearing, she quietly and calmly tells him she'll talk with him when he quiets down and stops swearing. She talks with him about what he's mad about when he quiets down and stops swearing.

To do this comfortably, confidently, and successfully requires developing three areas. The first, and most important, is how to act physically. Next is how to speak to him. Last, and least important, is what to say. Practice and build the skills in these three areas and a become a dragon-tamer. Find the "soft belly" of the dragon and save everyone misery and heartache.

The primary focus is on physical activity. It is where the dragon's attention is, what he senses and interacts with. He is acutely aware of your body state: the inner condition and outer action. Is there a relaxed or stressed condition? Are your buttons going off and you're going to lose your sense of yourself on the inside and play win/lose on the outside? What he will do next is based on your body state.

Body condition is composed of interior space—what is happening inside of you—and exterior space, what you are doing physically on the outside. The outside space, physical action, is determined by the conditions of the inside space. Interior space is where to start.

Developing the power of managing your interior space begins with breathing. As simple and trite as it may seem, breath is the energetic basis of strength, agility, and effectiveness in martial arts. It is the core of the most clinically successful stress management/reduction program in the country, a central skill in pain relief, and is used in training for negotiations, mediation, and conflict resolution. It saves people from losing their tempers.

Breath is full and natural, so that the belly button rises when you inhale and falls when you exhale. The illustrations below demonstrate "belly breathing."

Figure 5

This is the activity of breathing necessary in relation to your dragon. Your body condition remains relaxed and comfortable. It is the body basis that frees you from the "stress response" and replaces it with the "relaxation-alert" response. Unfortunately, the "stress response" is so common and automatic in our culture, that our usual breathing is shallow and strained with the chest and/or shoulders rising when we inhale instead of the belly. Dragons recognize this body state naturally and exploit it.

A dragon-tamer develops full and natural breath through practice. Simple, repetitious, practice. It's best to begin by placing your hand on your belly while laying down so the hand rises when you inhale and falls when you exhale.

Figure 6

Practice relaxed and natural breath while you're sitting, perhaps watching television, at a desk, driving a car, reading a book: anywhere seated, put your hand over the belly button and let it rise when you inhale and fall when you exhale. Next practice belly breathing standing, like in the kitchen, an elevator, on the golf course, in line at the post office—anywhere that you're standing. Now, add to your practice breathing naturally and fully while you're moving around. Lastly, make it the natural basis of breathing when you're around your boy. Breathing full and relaxed with your belly rising when you inhale and falling when you exhale always in the presence of your son.

The next skill in developing the power of your inner space is cultivating a sense of positive goodness that he cannot rattle. Creating a steady sense of inner goodness comes from your inward attention on a person, place, memory, and/or object that makes your "heart smile." Inwardly bringing it into your attention accesses an embodied felt sense that is "good" and "positive." It protects you from the fight/flight stress response, helping to maintain a centered sense of yourself.

The fight/flight stress response is deeply ingrained in our being. Dragons have practiced and honed their skills at pushing your buttons. Practicing a "smiling heart" diligently and patiently will pay off in augmenting the "stress response" and "re-wiring" your buttons to become a relaxed, centered dragon-tamer.

Follow the same practice model as belly breathing. Begin with when you are quietly laying down. Bring to mind what makes your "heart smile" to feel its affect wash over (embody) you. Add to your practice when you are sitting, then standing, moving and in the presence of your teenage son. Repetition is the key to practice becoming habit without thought.

The third skill for developing control of your inner space is the "anchor" awareness that you are in charge of yourself. That is your job! Out of that job comes your parenting skills. It destroys the attitude "he has all of the power" and activates the body/mind truth: you are in charge of yourself. This is modeling what a boy needs to develop his ability to be in charge of himself.

The attitude that teenage boys have all kinds of power to control their parents is rampant. It permeates the media, marketing, and many institutions. Your dragon has learned to set you off, to get under your skin with behavior that makes him feel like he's in charge of you. He needs you to stop letting him do that. Practicing the anchor awareness that you are in charge of yourself with commitment and repetition expands a calm, relaxed, centered sense of yourself and the ability to engage your dragon effectively.

Make "I am in charge of myself" an inner "mantra," affirmation, or prayer you practice over and over again, allowing the words to penetrate and embody you completely. Even when thoughts say, "No you're not," just keeping repeating, "I am in charge of myself." You are developing a new thought pattern and body awareness.

Practice initially when you're lying down. Add when you are sitting, then standing, next moving around, and finally in the presence of your boy. Repetition, over and over again, like it is the most important belief in the world. You might find that you laugh inwardly to yourself as you recognize more and more deeply the truth of this anchor awareness.

The final skill in cultivating your inner space is accepting this fact: there is nothing to be afraid of. He's just a boy trying to grow into a young man. He truly has no control over you.

Add "I am unafraid" to your thoughts. Practice . . . practice . . . practice. Diligently. Repeatedly. Like your life depends on it. When you're laying down, when you're sitting up, when you're standing, when you're moving around, and when you're in the presence of your son.

He is trying, through his inept behavior, to create change. Changing your inner space, your experience of yourself on the inside, is the alchemical condition that will allow you to perform magic tricks with your dragon.

From your interior space come the actions of your exterior space: the physical behavior visible on the outside, which boys are watching very carefully. The fundamental rule is comfortableness. It guides and informs everything you do. Every movement is intentionally comfortable, relaxed, and easy. Out of your comfortableness, you manage the space between you and your boy, changing it, if necessary, to remain comfortable and in control of your inner space.

Every relationship has a spatial quality to it: the distance between the people. That spatial quality has a feel to it: good or bad, relaxed or tense, safe or unsafe. Comfortable means you feel good, relaxed, and safe. It means your movements feel good, relaxed, and safe, and your interior space sense remains positive and good. Anything other than comfortable requires creating distance and controlling the space by moving away.

A simple exercise illustrates the subtle power and importance of how you act physically. Pay attention to how close or how far away from your boy you normally stand when you're with him. The next time you're in the same room, increase the space slightly. Move away. Why? From years of living with you, he has figured out what your "how you act physically" patterns are and has adapted what he does to them to get the results he wants! He feels in control and will act to control the space to maintain the pattern and to accomplish his goals. Being slightly further away changes the pattern, places you in control of the space, signals to him something is different, and allows you room to be effective in engaging him. He may shift his position to accommodate the change by moving closer, saying something to you, or possibly leaving the room because he is uncomfortable.

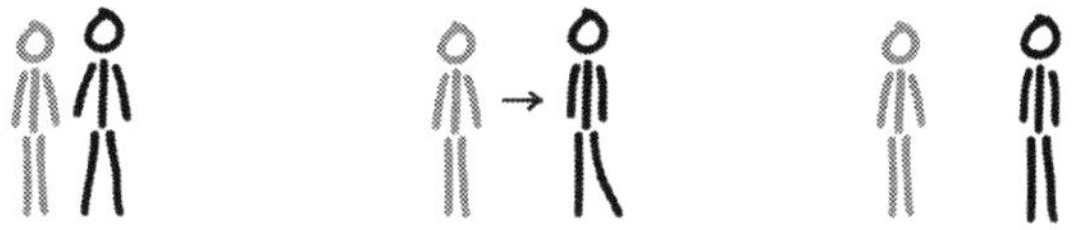

Figure 7

Being comfortable is the guiding principle for your actions and behavior with your teenage son. Practice being comfortable and managing the space between you and him whenever you are around him! All the time. Over and over again. It may be a challenge! He might think or say you're acting weird or different. Just shrug it off with a "whatever" or "really?" Allow it to become a way of being with him so when conflict occurs you can remain comfortable and in charge of the space between you and him. Now you're not trying to control what he does: you're controlling what you do.

Conflict will happen. He will act to push your buttons. Claim your space, set your rules of engagement, and act.

Your space is a place in the room that is your spot. You own it. You are comfortable and in control of the distance between you and him, applying all of your interior space skills. Your rules of engagement are the terms by which you will interact with him. These are the conditions under which you will deliver your message and talk with him. They are not negotiable. That may mean your rules of engagement are to stop speaking and listening to him for a while because you need time to recover. So be it. You're in charge of yourself. Take a break. The rules of engagement are the basis for maintaining your comfortableness and effectiveness. Action is your message and conversation.

Claiming your space, setting your rules of engagement, and acting require physical movements. You can stand your ground: stay in your spot. Don't move unless it's necessary to maintain your comfortableness and control the space between you and the dragon. He may move around, even forward. It's no big deal as long as you're relaxed and comfortable. It's about you, not him.

Figure 8

If he moves forward to close the space, you may move forward slightly. Chances are he'll move back.

Figure 9

Or, you may move away, creating distance, claim a new spot, and continue the action if you are comfortable.

Figure 10

In the special case where he is moving forward into your space, like about to get right in your face, if you are not comfortable standing your ground or moving slightly forward, you may step behind. Stepping behind involves a circular movement. As he gets close to you, move slightly forward toward him, turn sideways right next to him (either on the right or the left) so you're facing the same direction, and continue turning, completing the circle, stepping behind and moving away from him. Claim a new space.

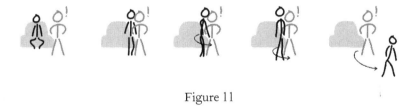

Figure 11

When finished, either because the interaction is complete, you're uncomfortable, or you might blow a gasket, step back. Leave the room and go somewhere else. The conversation is done for the time being. You're not offering an opportunity to interact now. Whenever the interaction is complete, step back and leave.

Should the interaction shift from conflict to a genuine listening interchange, move to sit side by side with him. It is a physical distance conveying interest, care, safety, and openness. Below the level of awareness, he'll sense how you've directed the interchange to a peaceful resolution. You will have modeled and allowed him to practice adult behavior.

Figure 12

There is a physical, spatial quality to relationships. It's visible in the physical space between people and how they move closer and further apart. Moving away from your son stretches an invisible "umbilical cord" connecting him to you, especially with his mother. He knows it by sensing it generally below the level of his awareness.

Your relaxed, comfortable physical presence and actions, managing the spatial relationship between your son and you, is 75% of the power in making a dynamic change with him. It is the area he is most focused on!

Born from the power of your physical sense is how you speak to him, how you deliver your message. Speak in a quiet, normal voice volume, tone, and pitch, with a sense of purpose and compassion, with love and care, like your son is precious to you, with truthful firmness and conviction: like you mean it. Your voice is the sound expression of the centered purposefulness of your interior and exterior space. Its quality conveys "I am at ease and there is nothing for me to argue."

He hears in your voice that you are comfortable and relaxed, certain of yourself, and neither threatened or belligerent with him.

The volume, pitch, and tone of your voice is as it would be for a normal conversation. No "extra" effort appears in how you speak. He has nothing to fight against and can begin to settle. How you speak is another 15% of the power in making a dynamic change with him.

Now we can begin to get to "what to say." What you do physically and how you speak are prerequisites because that is what he is focused on. He won't begin to pay attention to what you say if your physical actions and how you speak threaten or engage him in a win/lose scenario.

What you say is about you. The focus, the subject of each sentence, is always you. Not your teenage son: you as parent. Each and every time. Each sentence is an "I" message about what is on your mind. It can include how you are feeling, what you expect, what you are going to do, and the choices you're going to make. You also identify his choices: the options available to him as a result of your position. Options for your boy are integral and absolutely necessary. He is free to choose his actions knowing fully what your position is and the expected actions you will take depending on his choice. This is the polar opposite of trying to get him to do something.

What you say, the content, contains the least amount of words to convey your message. The purpose of as few words as possible will be clear in the next chapter, "Nothing For Free." Stick to your message. Do not deviate from it. Repeat it word for word if necessary. It is the verbal equivalent of "standing your ground." What you say is about you.

Here are two different conflict scenarios. The first is an active conflict: a full-blown dragon eruption. He's yelling and screaming that his clothes aren't washed and he doesn't have anything to wear. You've "claimed your space" and are ready to go.

"I'm not comfortable with the yelling and shouting at me. I'm willing to talk about the clothes when the loudness stops. Lower your voice and I'll talk about the clothes or keep shouting and I won't. Either way is OK with me."

The parent described what was on her/his mind and how he/she was feeling. She/he stated her/his position and described what she was going to do. Finally, the choices available were presented.

If you are very comfortable and confident with yourself, you can add this precursor before stating what is on your mind: acknowledge his feelings or views.

"I understand you're angry because you don't have any clothes, right?" He'll say "Yeah, probably," with a bunch of other nonsense.

Once he acknowledges agreement, move on to "what's on your mind?" You may have to repeat this precursor more than once before he acknowledges you understand him.

Tim was a sixteen-year-old dragon who swore like a sailor. One day, he was swearing and shouting at his mom, " I want to use the f . . king car on Friday." Mom looked at him, smiled and said, "Oh, swear at me, no car. Don't swear at me you can use the car. Either way is OK with me," and walked away.

The next example is a passive conflict. He leaves his clothes all around the house. Here's what you can say: "I'm not happy with the clothes all over the house. I want them picked up and put away within an hour. Picking them up and putting them away means you'll be able to keep using them. If they're still there in an hour, I'll gather them up and get rid of them. So you can pick them up and have them or I'll gather them up and remove them. Either way is OK with me, sweetheart."

She began with what was on her mind. Next was what she wanted or expected, and what choices she was going to make. Finally, what were the options or choices available to him.

Phrases that are good to say and will do the job include:

"Here's what I think and/or am willing to do . . . "
"Here's what's possible (if anything is), otherwise . . . "
"That doesn't work for me (or, this works better for me) . . . "
"I'm not comfortable with that (or, I'm more comfortable with) . . . "

Imagine yourself engaged with your teenage son while breathing naturally and feeling at ease, with a stance and posture coming out of that comfortableness that expresses being centered and grounded, with enough distance between you and him, speaking in a normal, matter-of-fact voice, volume, and pitch (can even have some warmth and tenderness), stating what is on your mind, what your expectations are, what choices you may make, what his options are, and leaving the room. Developing and applying the power to manage your inner and outer space, to control how you speak, and to deliver your message with inclusive warmth, compassion, and acceptance for everyone involved in conflicts with your dragon will tame him and open the portal for his maturing into a young man.

Becoming a "dragon-tamer" parent requires practice. It is common sense that getting good and skillful requires repetition. Your son is a master gamesman with you because he practices his moves on you all the time and over a number of years. Your advantage is knowledge, wisdom, and perspective. Another advantage is that his development is depending on you—and he is prepared to respond once he's certain your change is real, that your dragon-taming skills are not a "technique" you try and abandon under pressure from him, or he can undermine or outlast you.

The best way to practice and develop dragon-taming skills is in the absence of conflict. That is, martial artists train in classes so that if they ever need to respond in a real-life situation, they can access the skills without thinking about them. Musicians practice their instruments and music so when it is time to perform, they can access the skills without thinking about them. Same is true for athletes.

Practice throughout each day. Practice away from your boy. Practice when you're around him. Practice the four steps so your inner body gets used to being relaxed, comfortable, and centered. Practice keeping a little more distance between him and you. Practice speaking in a natural voice, volume, pitch, and tone. Practice speaking with as few words as possible. Practice so that when a conflict occurs you've got some experience under your belt, you can go into action and do your best.

Your boy is going to give you lots of opportunities to practice. Each event, each conflict is an opportunity to practice and hone your skills. He has to challenge you: his development depends on it. He does not know what else to do. Win/lose games is what he knows. He has to discover that the changes in you are real and lasting. Then he changes. He feels safe—you are really in charge of yourself and the conflict. He can relax, let go, and move on to the path of young manhood.

View each challenge, each conflict situation, as an opportunity to practice. Hone your skills each time, learn from your mistakes, get better so you continue to improve. It will enhance your success!

A great pitfall in becoming a dragon-tamer is "trying," as in "I tried but it did not work. He kept misbehaving." If you "try," and then revert to reactions and win/lose games when your fire-breathing dragon challenges you to find out if you've really changed or not, and you throw in the towel (instead of getting better at it), then he's not going to change because he's figured out how to get you to quit and get back into his game. That's his job: to find out if you're serious and real about being different.

Repetition, persistence, making mistakes—and sometimes failing. It's part of the practice learning curve. It's how you get better at dragon taming with power, conflict, love, and modeling for your teenage son.

Another common pitfall is "I'm a failure." One of the downsides to parent education is parents get a lot of information and understanding, then beat themselves up when they make a mistake and think they're a failure.

You're not a failure. You're courageous because you're willing to change. You're going to make mistakes. Everyone does when practicing and developing new skills. Mistakes are part of the practice and part of the learning process; not marks of failure. Accept them. Learn from them and keep going. You will get better at mastering yourself and taming your dragon.

You are learning to create more love. Literally, create more Love in the face of adversity. The crap that he pitches at you arouses anger, hurt, resentment, frustration in you. You are learning to find, feel, and act on the infinite Love inside of you instead of being pulled into the abyss of misery and suffering. That form of Love is more powerful than hurt, fear, and anger. That is the Power and Love that can be created from the cauldron of Conflict.

It is a challenging practice. The diamond in the coal is that human beings are born to be able to develop this capacity. Love the boys with the practice so they can learn it for themselves and mature into young men.

Part IV

Nothing For Free

Nothing For Free

For a teenage boy, everything is about power. With the onset of puberty, he stands at the threshold to move from the elementary level of power as control and domination to the practice of mastering himself. Power in an emerging young man requires developing his capacities, potentials, skills, talents, and abilities to make his way in the real world: to be purposeful, productive, and passionate in his life. To be successful on this path, he must not be able to steal someone else's power.

Parents are often exhausted after an eruption with their dragon. He's fine: they're wasted. He's stolen their power, literally sucked up their life energy. A boy becoming a young man cannot be able to get away with crap, especially getting something he wants from someone else without putting anything into the relationship.

For teenage boys on the path of manhood, nothing is for free.

Historically, everything about a child's development was to prepare him to function successfully and support the survival of his culture/society. For boys, that meant a rite of passage: an initiation process that separated him from the rest of society and subjected him to a series of ordeals and tests to demonstrate his readiness and prepare him in the ways of being a man in his society. He'd leave a boy and return a young man with an adult role and something to contribute to his group.

Contemporary American society does not have a functioning coming-of-age procedure for its boys. Male arrival at maturity now occurs somewhere around the age of 26–35, long after boys are biologically and developmentally ready to become men. The disparity between the developmental potential in boys and their social/cultural context throughout the teenage years produces enormous problems.

Aspects of the coming-of-age process must be woven into his family life. He has to have different relationships with his parents as a teenager than he had as a boy, and he has to earn his freedom and demonstrate his ability to handle power through his behavior, including making a contribution to his "tribe," the family.

Part of being a man in the world is contributing your labor, earning your keep, your livelihood. A teenage boy has to practice in order to be good and prepared. He cannot develop confidence if he does not earn it through his own efforts and without demonstrating his abilities. The truth is he is deeply ready to take on this task.

The task mandates that nothing is for free, especially and including attention.

To a teenage boy, every word out of your mouth is a unit of attention, a ten-dollar bill he deposits in his account. This fact totally confounds parents who are trying to get their son to do something simple and reasonable, but viewed through his eyes, it makes perfect sense.

In his boy world, he wants attention and is used to getting it from your behavior. He's been around you his whole life and he knows exactly what you're going to do and say to him. Whatever you do and say is attention to him. Usually, what you provide is more than enough to meet his needs (and then some). He receives the units of attention "free of charge," requiring nothing more from him than his normal behavior. For him, usually without being aware of it, it's a game he wins by getting the attention he's used to, simply by being his normal, teenage self.

In this game, every word out of your mouth is a unit of loving attention, your human energy, he absorbs. And he will steal, I mean rob you blind of your units of attention by pushing your buttons and setting off a win/lose game or a version of "what can I get away with." That is why you feel so exasperated and drained after a fight with him. He's stolen your power.

Much of the time, he steals it and you don't even know it because you're just talking to him the way you've always talked to him since he was a little boy: blathering away about this and that, asking him questions ("How was your day?" "What did you do?" "Do you have any homework?"), to which you get mono-syllabic responses at best, if you get anything verbal. The parent is doing all of the talking.

It's stealing when he either puts nothing into the equation to get your attention because you do all of the talking, or he sets up a heist: pushing your buttons, setting off a win/lose game so you'll go off on him while he pockets all of the units of attention.

He does not care that it is negative attention because he's already learned he gets more units of attention for doing something "wrong" that doing something "right" (because that is what is expected, so why should he get attention for it?).

He also does not care because it does not require anything developmental from him to get the attention. Any little boy can pull it off. Push a button: *ka-ching*! The slot machine pays the bonanza each time. Why should he stop doing that?

His game. His rules. You pay out. He does not grow up. He'll complain about you to high heaven and to all of his friends but will not lead the way to change the situation. He's a boy: he's not going to come to you and ask, "Can I have some attention please?"

If he can steal someone else's power, he stays a boy. Developmentally, he needs the adults to not let him steal their power and rob them of units of attention. He needs adults to control the flow of attention based on what is developmentally appropriate and correct for him to grow into a young man.

To start, the simple formula is: talk less. You be in charge of the units of attention—when and how you give them. Go about the business of your life. Focus your attention on yourself. Be casual, warm, friendly, and don't talk with him. When you speak with him, be brief and and keep your attention on yourself, not on him.

If you have something to say and can get your message stated in three words, then use three words, not thirty. Think before you speak. What is the message you intend to deliver? Craft the delivery in as few of words as possible. In keeping with putting the dynamics of power, conflict, and love into practice, structure your sentences as "I" statements: where you are the subject of the sentence, not your boy. Be brief and simple. Be warm and true.

When you're in his presence, if he does not talk, neither do you. Focus on yourself. Involve yourself in something you want or need to do. If necessary, go into a different room. If you're in the car, listen to your station(s) on the radio or sing or hum to yourself; whistle "Dixie."

The purpose is to turn off the tap of attention that he has been thriving on, drawing whatever he wants without putting anything into the relationship. You're going to control the tap: turn it on and off as is developmentally appropriate for him.

This is the reason why in the previous section, "Putting It Into Practice," in the section of "how you say it" and "what you say," I suggested that you speak with as few of words as possible. For your son to begin to develop into a young man, it is necessary that you, not he, control the units of attention he receives.

Your boy is going to start coming around looking for attention. Good! When he starts a conversation, let him do the talking. Reverse the roles: he talks, you listen. Listening, understanding, and appreciating him are more appropriate and effective parenting skills in developing a young man than talking to him. Allow him to engage and invest in the relationship. Practice brevity in your speech and pay attention to him with as few words as possible!

A mom in a "Ferocious Love: Dragon Taming for Mothers of Teenage Boys" class told this story. Normally, she barrages her high school boy with talk and a multitude of questions when she picks him up from school. He says nothing back to her. This time, she picked him up from school and simply said "hello" to him. That's all. After a few minutes, her son asked, "Mom, are you mad about something?" She answered, "No, why?" He responded, "Well, did something happen at work that upset you?" Her reply was, "No." Quiet for awhile after her answer. Then her son said, "Mom, can I hold your hand please?" to which she answered, "Yes." He reached over to hold her hand and said, "Mom, I love you and I want you to know how much I appreciate everything you do."

Another mom in the workshop, a self-professed "talker" offered her story. She and her teenage boys were preparing to carve the pumpkins for Halloween. Normally, she'd be talking up a storm telling them to "do this" and "do that" and on and on. Instead, she said next to nothing and hummed a little bit. The boys filled the space, talking with her, each other, and enjoying the pumpkin carving.

When they finished, one son said, "Mom, this was the best time. Thank you so much!"

What a teenage boy needs developmentally is a different form of attention than what he had as a boy. He needs listening and understanding, attention focused on what he is talking about. And he will not talk if you are supplying all of the attention by talking yourself. It is not being cold, cruel or abandoning him. It is creating a space for him to grow, to become more maturely present on the family stage, to show himself more fully. You have the opportunity to engage and model adult relating so he can learn to do it himself.

He cannot move into this space if it does not exist. He will not change as long as you relate to him in the manner that he is used to, because an invisible, but critical, factor in a dragon's win/lose games is that he is very successful. He gets lots of units of attention for his misbehavior and other shenanigans. He will set you up, push your buttons, even play "good boy" to get his units of attention. Once he has them, he's going to turn you off! He gets them for free, literally stealing your energy. When you're doing all or most of the talking, he is winning, you are losing. He's not growing into a young man; you're frustrated and drained.

To create this space: talk less. Speak with as few of words as possible. Let him do the talking. Allow him to engage and invest in the relationship. Listen, understand and appreciate more, talk less.

Besides attention, boys acquire activities, services, objects of desire, symbols of power, and fragments of freedom for free. In contemporary America, teen boys feel they are entitled to just about everything. The cultural context, media, and marketplace create this condition and provide a plethora of objects the boys want. It flies in the face of reality of what they need to grow into young men. It sets the stage for vast amounts of anger, frustration, pain, and grief for parents and sons.

Developmentally, when a boy comes into adolescence, when he turns the corner onto the path of young manhood, he is ready and able to apply his knowledge, skills, and abilities in the world. Biologically, he is ready to make a contribution *and* experience the satisfaction and power that comes from earning his way. Historically, a rite of passage/initiation process occurred to test his readiness and prepare and transform him into young man. Without initiation, a boy moves through adolescence without developing into a young man, coming into adulthood unprepared.

Not only is the absence of initiation against his best interests, he's going to drive you crazy because he will continuously play boy games to get what he wants: entrapping you into playing the games with him, frustrating you and draining your energy.

A boy must earn his way in becoming a young man: in his relationship exchanges, in acquiring symbols and objects of power, and in exercising freedom. Once a boy reaches early adolescence: nothing is for free. This isn't mean or cruel. It is an intentional and determined act of love allowing him to develop his strength and power, his confidence in himself.

Consider these three areas: his relationship exchanges, getting something he wants, or an extension of his freedom. He wants it all for free, or to get away with as little effort as possible (a version of "what can I get away with").

In his relationship exchanges, he wants to either to be able to do something and/or for you to do something for him. Normally, he just wants to be able to do it and for you to just do whatever he wants. For example, he wants to go to a friend's house and wants you to drive him. Driving him is giving up your time in order to do something for him. Applying "nothing for free" means he does something to contribute to the household/family in exchange for the ride to his friend's.

Boy: Mom, will you drive me to Sammy's house?
Mom: I'll drive you to Sammy's house after the clothes are picked up off the floor in the bedroom and put away where they belong.

The rule still applies if the situation doesn't require something of you, only he wants to do something. Nothing for free: there is something you want in exchange.

Boy: Mom, can I go to Sammy's house?
Mom: I'm OK with it after the clothes are picked up from the floor and put away.

He gets the green light after he's earned it: after he's put something into the equation.

Here's the story of a deal a boy made with his mother after they had moved to a new community. The boy was thirteen, and wanted his mom to drive him to his old neighborhood all the time to see his friends. Mom, who worked long hours running a customer service department, wanted him to complete his school work and turn it in. They fought about it constantly. After kindly confronting the boy that, despite his claims, he really did not want to do his homework, a deal was struck. Mom agreed to drive her son to see his friends once a week and on the weekends when he demonstrates to her that his school work was complete, turned in, and received credit.

Nothing is for free! When he wants something from you, if it is something you are truly willing to do, make a deal with him in which he is exchanging something of his (labor and getting a job done) for something of yours (time and effort).

Why? Because that is how the adult world operates. As a young man-in-the-making, he needs training and practice in functioning in the adult world. He needs to prepare for what he is facing or be stuck in boyhood in a bigger body. He needs to be treated as a young man to in order to become a young man. He already has plenty of practice with the make-believe world where he feels, and experiences, that he's entitled to A, B, and C effortlessly.

When he wants you to get him something for him: nothing is for free. Let's say he wants to play guitar and have lessons. Or a skate board. Or a bicycle. It is his developmental job to do the research and investigation. It is his job to figure out how to earn the money. It is his job to finish, adapt, or discard the project. Your job is to support him doing his jobs.

Boy: Dad, I want to play guitar. I need a guitar and lessons.
Dad: Hmmm . . . start with investigating the guitars and the places that offer lessons. Come back with the information, including costs, and I'll talk about it.

A couple of days later the boy returns:

Boy: Dad, I want a Gibson Les Paul custom. The Guitar Center downtown has them for $1200.00. They also have lessons there. They cost $40.00 per half hour. When can we go?
Dad: Gibson Les Paul custom for $1200.00. How will the money be earned to pay for the guitar?

Boy: That's a lot of money Dad! I don't know how I can earn that much money.

Dad: OK. Think about it. I think you're good at problem solving and I know when you really want something, you figure out how to do it. I'm supporting you getting a guitar and lessons.

This can go several ways: the fundamental does not change. Nothing is for free. If he wants something enough, he'll figure out a way to earn the money to buy it. In the process, he may adjust what he wants to meet the reality he's facing. He may choose a less expensive item. He may delay the purchase. He may discard the idea completely, in which case it was not that important to him. A good lesson for all of you.

Whatever the outcome, he's accomplished it. He's earned the money and bought the item. He's adjusted what he wants and earned the money to buy it. He's decided to forgo the item. His choice. And you've parented him to experience that process again and again so he becomes comfortable and confident functioning in this adult reality.

Billy was a thirteen-year-old boy who wanted an ATV. He asked his dad to buy him one. Dad responded similarly to the guitar story: do the research on "four-wheelers," including costs. The boy came back with the make and model he wanted and the price. Dad asked him how he'd earn the money to buy it. Billy left the room dismayed. A couple of days later he told his Dad that he decided to put off getting an ATV because it was not worth it to him to spend that much money on one.

When he wants you to get him something, support his wanting the something, but not your getting it for him. Support his doing the research and investigation. Support his problem solving. Support his earning the money. Celebrate his accomplishing his goal or deciding to let it go. He is building his young manhood and you are helping him along his way.

Finally, he wants an extension of his freedom in the form of time or a "mode of power." Teenage boys say they want more freedom, they want to make their own choices, to run or live their own lives. They're in constant friction with their parents about "who's in charge of them." They also want a cell phone, a driver's license, and all of the other goodies that belong to grown-ups. The conventional wisdom is, give it to them. Once they're "old enough," they should be able to acquire these "modes of power."

But age is irrelevant. "With great power comes great responsibility" (Benjamin Parker in *The Amazing Spider-Man*). Being ready is relevant.

As a martial artist, it is wrong to give a weapon to a trainee unless he practices and demonstrates the ability to handle the weapon properly. My hunting friends do not allow their boys to fire a rifle and hunt without proper training and showing he has the skills to be safe. The training and set of tests or ordeals is an initiation he must complete that requires a level of maturity in skill, behavior, and judgment before he's allowed into that "society." He earns it: nothing is for free.

In reality, it is no different with any other powerful item.

First, a "mode of power," like a cell or smart phone. You may disagree, but a cell phone is not a child's toy, even though it is marketed as something that every kid should have and something the parents should get them because they're cool, they need one, and the companies make it inexpensive and help the parents to adapt their thinking to believe their boy needs one so the parents can keep in touch with him.

A cell phone is a mode of power that used to come with adult status. It gives the boys the power to keep in touch with their peers, a form of communication, especially through texting, that is invisible to the grown-up world unless a conscientious effort is made to access it. It is also a mode of power to navigate being in the world. It becomes an extension of who he is and how he gets along in the world. He can be in the world in ways his parents are excluded. The question: is he ready for that degree of power?

Cell phones are one more item, along with an array of electronic devices, that are fodder for the family win/lose fights and "what can I get away with" games. They're also an opportunity to develop and demonstrate his young manhood. What you do with him will set the stage for that opportunity.

Boy: Mom, I want a cell phone. Everyone has one and I feel stupid not having one.
Mom: It may be possible. Check out phones and costs and come back to me.

The next day he's back.

Boy: Mom, I want an Android phone. They're $300.00 with a calling and data plan. What do you think? Can I get one?
Mom: How will you earn the money to buy it? What is the monthly cost? How will you pay it?

Boy: Won't you buy it for me?
Mom: This is something you want. The right thing is to earn it and pay for it yourself.

Next day he's back.

Boy: Mom, I've decided on a phone that is $75.00 and I think we can just add it to our cell phone plan for $10.00 a month.
Mom: How will you earn the money to buy the phone? Also, the

monthly charge depends on how many minutes each month you use the phone, because our plan has a fixed number of minutes to it.

Boy: I have $20.00 saved up. I have plans to cut two neighbors' lawns tomorrow which will earn $40.00. Then I'll cut our lawn over the weekend for the remaining $15.00. I'll pay the $10.00 per month from lawn cutting or snow removal in the winter.

Mom: OK . . . here's the deal. I'll agree to a three-month trial period with these conditions. You may buy the phone. You will pay $10.00 for your line plus $15.00 per month to pay for additional minutes on our plan plus the taxes and service charges. Any over-charges are paid by you. Payment is due on the first of the month. Unpaid charges suspends the phone. Access to the phone is only during waking hours; use after bedtime suspends the phone. Near the end of the trial period, we'll evaluate if this is working or not. If you're keeping your end of the deal, we'll continue. If you're not, we'll re-evaluate and possibly stop the phone.

Boy: Deal.

Now, this scenario assumes the boy is already behaving in a developmentally appropriate way with you. So, what if he's not? What if he's a full-scale dragon leaving his crap around the house, mouthing off, skipping his schoolwork and being a royal pain in the behind?

Boy: Mom, I want a cell phone. Everyone has one and I feel stupid not having one.
Mom: A cell phone. What do you have in mind?

Boy: I want the new Android. It's very cool and lots of my friends have one.
Mom: OK, here's the deal. When I see clothes and other items you use cleaned up and put away regularly, your school work is completed to the best of your ability and turned in on time, and I

don't hear you mouthing off to me, I'll talk with you about getting a cell phone.

Boy: Mom, that's ridiculous. You're being an idiot. Nobody has to do that to get a cell phone. Everybody else has one. You want me to look like a fool. You don't care about me with your stupid rules.
Mom: Sounds like you don't like the idea. My view is a cell phone is powerful and gives you power. I'm waiting to see that you can handle that power.

Boy: What are you talking about? You're so stupid!
Mom: Hmmm. OK. When I see your clothes and other items you use cleaned and put away regularly, your school work is completed to the best of your ability and turned in on time, and I don't hear you mouthing off to me, I'll talk with you about getting a cell phone.

An extension of his freedom: a later curfew, perhaps, or the ability to come and go as he pleases without providing any information as to his whereabouts. Maybe a job outside of the house. All are linked to an "initiation"—a demonstration of his readiness to handle the freedom, power and responsibility that come with them. It is not a given by virtue of his age. It is bestowed as a recognition of his readiness. Providing something for him without his earning it, without an "initiation," is asking for trouble, delays his development and maturity, and is going to cause you a lot of grief!

Boy: Dad, I want a job. I need the money. My friend can get me in at the pizza shop in town.
Dad: I'm willing to talk about a job after you keep your room and the rest of the house clean of your stuff, your school work is done, turned in and given credit, and you stop picking on your sister.

Boy: What! You've got to be kidding. That's the stupidest thing I ever heard. What's all that have to do with getting a job? I told you, I need the money.

Dad: I understand. I'm willing to talk about a job after you keep your room and the rest of the house clean of your stuff, your school work is done, turned in and given credit, and you stop picking on your sister.

Boy: I can't believe it! You're serious?

Dad: Yes. I think a job is a great idea.

Boy: So, I can get one?

Dad: I'm willing to talk about a job after you keep your room, and the rest of the house, clean of your stuff, your school work is done, turned in and given credit, and you stop picking on your sister.

It does not matter what the mode of power or extension of freedom is. He wants driver's education and his license? Nothing for free. It is necessary for him to demonstrate his readiness, not simply the skills of driving a car, but as importantly, his power to exercise safety, withstand peer pressure, and use good judgment.

The actions of "nothing for free" emerge from the skills developed in "Putting It Into Practice," allowing your son to experience being treated differently by you, relating to him as a young man so he can grow into one. Once he reaches puberty: nothing is for free. For his sake. For your sake. For everyone's sake.

PART V

PURPOSE, MISSION, AND DREAMS

PURPOSE, MISSION, AND DREAMS

At the heart of a teenage boy is at least one dream: a seed of his purpose. It drives him forward. It is the source of his mature power: the embodied sense of his own authority from which he directs his actions. Hidden within his boredom and fear, avoided by his rebellious win/lose games, and fueling his craving for challenge and responsibility that are real and meaningful to him, are dreams of who he'd like to be and things he'd like to do.

On the surface, his dream, when he or anyone else is aware of it, will look as if it comes from something in society or our culture. Below the surface, his dream comes from the invisible realm of his psyche. The ancient Greeks referred to his *daimon* and the Romans to his *genius*: the inherently unique, what they considered divine, nature that is present in every boy and drives him forward into the future.

His dream is directly connected to this inherently unique character. His development, his growing into the man he is meant to be, fulfilling his mission and purpose in life, his destiny, begins with his dream.

It is not a straight path. Very few in life are straight. Still it is his path; and his confidence, maturity, and power grow and gain strength through developing his dreams: the work and play of making them come true, the activity of knowing who he is and being who he is in the world.

Frequently, teenage boys hide their dreams. When grown-ups view teenage boys as "problems" and whacko with testosterone and other common myths, they miss the deeper truth: he is a boy trying to become a young man—and as a young man, he wants and needs to accomplish something. That something is his purpose and the first sign of purpose is his dream.

Boys fool the grown-ups by playing the roles prescribed by the common myths. They are masters at manipulating the myths grown-ups have about them, at deception and distraction to avoid being aware and talking openly about their dreams. They are afraid! They unwittingly participate in denying they have them, and act out being the problem boys.

Parents remark, "My son no more has a purpose or dream than I'm ready to fly to the moon. He just wants to sit around and play video games or socialize or talk with his girlfriend or watch TV." Yes, he's doing that, and no, there is more going on inside of him—but he won't show it. He will fulfill the "problem child" image to his detriment and yours.

A common problem-child image is the "lazy slacker" watching television and movies, playing video games, doing minimal to no schoolwork, and lousy grades. Colin is a fifteen-year-old with a 1.7 grade point average halfway through his sophomore year of high school. He says he's had counseling before and doesn't need it now. What he does want is to become an engineer after attending a university in northern Michigan. A 1.7 GPA isn't going to get him into that school. He decides getting help to make his dream come true is necessary and important.

What drives boys forward into their futures are their dreams. What they regret the most is not living them, giving them a shot, going for them. Later as men, the lost opportunity fills them with sadness and regret, often for the rest of their lives.

The whole course of male adolescence can be viewed as a rite of passage period: where the boy is propelled forward facing challenges, ordeals, and adventures that transform him into the man he is meant to be. The internal pushing forward is his unique self wanting to become, his internal motivation. It is attached to his dreams of what he'd like to do, who he'd like to be, what makes him tick.

Charley was a thirteen-year-old having run-ins with other kids in his middle school and quite a challenge to his parents. He avoided talking about what was important to him until he blurted out angrily, "You want to know what I'm really interested in? I'll tell you. Aviation. Planes and helicopters. But I won't be able to be successful because I'm near-sighted and I can't become a fighter pilot." When he found out there is state-supported university in Michigan with an aviation program where he could graduate in aviation technology, including having his pilot's license, he shouted, "I want to go there!"

Fulfilling dreams requires training, the active involvement of adults who know and understand the process, and know-how to engage with him as he pursues the path of making his dream come true. What drives teenage boys nuts is feeling lost, confused, afraid, uncertain who they are: where they are going and what they are going to be.

Yet, it is seemingly impossible to get the training. Teenage boys live a paradox: everything is about power but they exercise it through "rebellious" win/lose games experiencing powerlessness because they cannot win even as they avoid losing at all costs. They are masters of deception, hiding what is really important to them in dragon games with their parents and other grown-ups. Their dreams will not appear amidst major family battles and win/lose games. A central role of the games is to distract from what is really important to them.

✤

Alvin was fifteen years old. Adopted from an east Asian country and born with cerebral palsy, he had special education support at his local public school. His parents discovered in the Individual Education Program (IEP) meeting the spring of his sophomore year of high school that his grades were terrible and he'd been lying to everyone about getting his work done. He ended up in my office.

Intelligent, charming, and articulate, he focused his attention on his school work and improving his grades. After several months of meetings, lo and behold his mid-term junior year grades were as bad as his sophomore grades. His parents were furious!

He sat in my office slouched over in his seat with his head hanging down expecting the usual grown-up confrontation/lecture. I looked at him and said curiously and caringly:

"What is it like to lie to the people you love the most?"

He sat up with his jaw hanging open. I repeated the question:

"What's it like to lie to the people you love the most?"

He looked directly at me and said:

"Ted, I'm a very private person and there are some things on my mind I don't tell anyone."

I looked back at him, nodding. He continued:

"I've been raised in a very good family. We have a good home, my parents love me and have provided and taken good care of me. I don't know if I'm going to be able to have that for myself. I don't know if I'll ever be able to have a good job or buy a house. Or get married: who's going to want to date me? Am I ever going to be able to have a girlfriend? I want a home and a family and I'm afraid I won't be able to have them."

He's crying.

Quietly nodding my head, with tears in my eyes, I said, "I understand. Let me help you so you can make those dreams come true."

His dream was to grow up and have a wife, family, home, and job. You'd never have known it from his behavior. Everything he did distracted the grown-ups, and himself, from what really mattered to him: his dream.

Teenage boys have a dream, a desire to become something, do something. The path of making the dream come true is strewn with obstacles and pitfalls, both internal and external. Traversing the path is man-in-the-making action. Parenting him on his path is a transformative gift and challenge.

Once you are shifting out of win/lose with him and are practicing managing your interior space, maintaining a comfortableness physically with him, speaking in a natural voice volume, tone, and pitch, stating your position, expectations, and choices with the least amount of words, and you're operating where nothing is free, you'll be able to begin an exploration with him about his dreams. You're going to be different. He's going to be different. You're going to be more able to listen to him seriously. He's going to be more comfortable talking with you.

Dream-making with dragons has four elements. The first is identifying the dream. It entails an open, safe, curious and accepting role for the parents, asking him simply what he dreams of doing now? What sparks his imagination? What is he interested in discovering, learning, exploring, being able to do, accomplish, or be? What would he like more of in his life?

Your job is to listen wholeheartedly and understand him. With respect, seriousness, and love. Write notes if it helps you. If you're not sure of something he's saying, tell him you didn't get it and ask him to say it again or tell him what you understand and ask him if you're right and understand him. It is critical and absolutely necessary that you truly understand him and he knows it.

When he's finished, re-state your understanding and get confirmation from him. When he says, "Yes, you've got it, you understand my dream," you are now allies in dream-making. You and he have identified the dream. Finish with re-stating the dream in a simple statement, one that is clear and easy to talk about.

There are some clues, signs, and symbols that may be helpful before you ask about his dreams. What does he like to do? Skateboard? Make films? Play a sport? Art, mechanics, electronics? How does he use his time without grown-up interference? What is he genuinely interested in? What are his talents and abilities? These questions can alert you to the possibilities of his dreams. It is just as likely he may have it completely hidden from view.

The second element is developing the path, a "road map" for pursuing the dream. The map has two primary points. The most important is the end point: the dream fulfilled. This is what it looks like and where he'll be when he's made his dream come true. The other is the starting point: where he is right now. Beginning to develop the path is an action he may do himself, or with you. With the end and the beginning in place, the sequential steps will appear later.

The same rules of conversation: love, respect, acceptance, patience, and understanding. You are his ally and advocate in developing the path, building his road map. He may want a representation of his map, an actual drawing showing the starting and end points, or some other physical and/or visual model of his quest.

With the start and end points of the map created, the question is, what comes next; what is the first step? He may ask. You may ask. Let him answer. Even if it takes him awhile. Be his advocate, not his answer. Once that question is answered, he's on his way.

Traversing the path is the dream making in action. Each step on the path will have its own ups and downs for him. Good! These are the realities engaging his "young man-in-the-making." They will require thought, reflection, decision-making, problem-solving, review and reconsideration. He'll face everything imaginable from successes to utter frustrations (perhaps failures) to both celebrate and overcome. Traversing the path creates healthy bodies, resilient minds, and strong souls. Each step leads to the next one; one step at a time.

It is likely he does not have, or believe he has, the skills necessary to realize the dream. Be his ally, a pillar of love and belief in him, a resource for him to draw upon in order to move forward. As he walks the path, he can review his progress with you and receive guidance and training in skills for facing challenges, obstacles, and resistance. It may require learning brainstorming, problem-solving, creative thinking, intuitive thought, reflection, introspection, and patience. You will be called upon to use all of the dragon-taming skills you've learned and become an expert listener, learning to empower him making his way along his path. Celebrate with him as he accomplishes steps. Commiserate with him when he hits obstacles, both external and internal. With your love and belief in him, he will make his way.

The fourth element is the dream come true and/or a new dream. He reaches the "end point" identified in "developing the path" to making his dream come true. He is no longer the same person as when he started. Honor and celebrate him. Have a ceremony bestowing blessing and recognition. Welcome him into the realm of a greater maturity and power. Allow him the opportunity to claim his accomplishments, to be proud of himself publicly. He is entitled to more freedom and responsibility. He has a different status in the family and community, deserving a greater voice and participation.

A new dream will emerge. Perhaps not immediately, but after a period of restfulness, consolidation, and incorporation, his soul will produce another dream with purpose and passion. The four elements of dream-making repeat. And so he begins anew along the spiral path of young man making.

It is entirely possible he will discard a dream. So be it. That is not the end of the journey, but a shift in direction, a change of course, the making of a new dream. He begins again carrying with him all of the knowledge, skills, and development he's acquired along the way. Honor and bless him. You are and remain a pillar of love and belief. It is his life he is creating, his movement into young manhood.

Your son's dream will first appear in early adolescence. His dream-making into young manhood builds the confidence and stamina needed to face the grand transition into adulthood: leaving home and making his way in the world. Dream-making builds the foundation from which his purpose emerges, pulling him forward into his life.

Throughout the entire dream-making process, your role as parents has two balanced elements: blessing and order. Blessing is being a pillar of love and acceptance of him without regard for the outcome. From the unconditional love you truly have for him, recognize that dream-making is your son's path in creating himself as a young man. The first blessing is recognizing he will have a dream and engaging him in identifying it. The second blessing is supporting his dream-making: being a resource for unconditional love, knowledge, skills, and expertise both within and outside the home that are necessary for pursuing the dream. You may offer validation for his actions and efforts.

For example, a boy has the dream of buying a truck. He got a job and has begun saving his money.

Boy: Dad, I've just deposited $500.00 in the bank and my balance is now $1725.00.
Dad: Congratulations! I'm glad for you. How are you feeling?

Boy: Great! Good. Strong, like I can do it.
Dad: Yes, I believe so.

Blessing includes acceptance of his trials and tribulations, successes and setbacks, with patience, understanding, and equanimity: all expressions of your unconditional love.

Dad: What's up. Not a happy face.
Boy: I got fired from work. I'm so pissed off. I was late a couple of times and he let me go. I didn't even get a chance.

Dad: I see. Now what?
Boy: I dunno. I'm just so mad at myself. And at him too. He could've given me a chance.

Dad: Uh huh.
Boy: What can I do. I don't think it's fair. What do you think I should do?

Dad: How can you solve this?
Boy: I dunno. I could go talk with him and ask for another chance and promise I'll never be late, that I'll be on time. Hell, I'll even be early and come in whenever he needs someone.

Dad: You could do that. Anything else?
Boy: If I can't get my job back, I'll have to find another job.

Dad: Yes, you can do that. I'm sure you can.

He will make his way moving forward, sliding backwards, and slipping sideways. Witness and honor your son assuming the task of dream-making, becoming a young man.

Order is the realm of rules and boundaries in participating in his dream-making. It is the when, the where, and, most important, the how you engage with your son while he traverses his path. Always engage from the power and love you're developing.

Within the realm of order are resources to offer as parent. You have knowledge, wisdom, experience, skills, and people that may be useful to him in his dream-making. You may offer resources to your son for him to accept or reject. Access to men who are already living the dream is invaluable in young man-making. Regular contact with other men, seeing how they do it, deeply awakens his own capacities.

You may make agreements with your son. An agreement is a task, activity, or practice that one or both of you voluntarily commit to in the service of his dream-making. For example, you may agree to meet once a month to review his progress. By the same token, you may agree to never meet to review his progress. You may agree to contact a person by a particular date. He may agree to finish some element of the dream and demonstrate it's complete. When you commit to an action, complete it in the agreed time frame. Defining agreements becomes part of the fabric of order.

Finally, order may include being a resource for observation, reflection, and confrontation. Confrontation is never attacking the person, as in "I'm confronting Johnny because he lied" or "I'm confronting Bill because he failed to keep his end of the bargain." Inner and outer body conditions, voice tone and volume, are critical in an effective confrontation: relaxed, comfortable, calm, and normal. The language is simple. Confrontation always focuses on the facts and is delivered from the point of view of the parent.

Dad: We didn't have our meeting this week to review your bank account.
Boy: I'm sorry Dad, I was playing frisbee golf with the guys and I forgot.

Dad: Really? First time that's happened. What's up?
Boy: Nothing Dad, I just forgot. Haven't you ever forgotten something?

Dad: Uh huh. So what's up?
Boy: I said, nothing.

Dad: So how's your account?
Boy: Well, not too good actually.

Dad: No?
Boy: I didn't put anything away this week.

Dad: What happened?
Boy: I dunno. I just spent it all. I don't even really know what I spent it all on.

Dad: Oh. How you feel about that?
Boy: Crappy. Really crappy. I'm pretty embarrassed and ashamed actually.

Dad: I understand. Now what?
Boy: I guess I get back on track.

Dad: Anything you want to differently?
Boy: Keep my promise and put away my money towards getting the truck.

Dad: How're you going to do that?
Boy: I can take my check to the bank and deposit the savings amount right away instead of having my boss cash my check at the store and later going to the bank.

Dad: OK. See how that works for you.

The intent is always to bring out into the open what is hidden and stuck. True to all conflicts, confrontation is an opportunity for something new and different to occur.

The boy's job is simple and challenging: to participate fully in the process.

The fifteen-year-old high school sophomore with the 1.7 average accepted the offer for help. It was not a cake-walk. Slowly, but steadily, he improved his grades, confronting his laziness along the way, and sharpening his learning skills. In the process, his parents witnessed a change in his behavior at home. His father gave him a fairly large job to do. Instead of procrastinating (his usual M.O.), he worked on it diligently each day for over three weeks until the task was done. He graduated with a 3.1 grade point average, was accepted to the technical university he wanted to attend, and his parents acknowledged and welcomed his success.

The thirteen-year-old is performing well in high school. The fifteen-year-old with cerebral palsy surprised himself in discovering he enjoyed learning and winning at the "game of school." He was accepted to and graduated from the college of his choice and has his first professional job.

CONCLUSION

Today, boys becoming men live on the threshold of a new era. The fundamental definition of man as superior to woman is in its death throes and, if we survive, a new form of man is coming into being. The chaos and confusion occurring at the end of this epoch impacts the boys enormously, at the very least creating a powerful downward pressure on their development. How do they become men if they cannot see the destination? How do the adults usher them into manhood when they're lost in the confusion?

The seed of the man coming into being lies inside each boy, harbored in his dream, waiting to set sail, his purpose and destiny unfolding through his journey on the sea of Life. Once he "crosses the bridge and enters the forest" of adolescence, it's a new beginning. He has the opportunity to bring the power, skills, and imagination he grew as a child into their adult forms, and to set aside pains and sufferings that would stop him. He requires adults—his parents and others— to see the invisible man in the boy and enable and empower him to follow his path. It is a hugely creative time full of peril and promise.

Ironically, adults do not, and often cannot, see clearly the man in the boy. They do not have to! What they have to do is know he is there, and that the boy wants to become him. What they have to do is provide, and if necessary create, the context for the man-in-the-making to become. That includes the necessity of embodying in themselves adult forms of power, conflict, and love. Each boy requires engagement with adults who are immune to a boy's win/lose games, who hold to their own truthful values and expectations with love and acceptance, and who empower him on the path of making his dreams come true.

Anything less will fail! Boys becoming the men they were born to become will either abort or be delayed well into midlife, and even then be in jeopardy without a significant catalyst that awakens them from their slumber. All of the seductions of contemporary society actively distract and deter men-in-the-making from coming into being. The later in life, the greater the challenge.

Collectively, we bear responsibility to shift our view of boys and become the adults they need to find their true way into manhood. Teenage boys are not problems. They are boys ready and trying to become young men. Their adolescence is a "second birth" exemplified by the enormous growth of brain material that occurs from late childhood into early adolescence. It is all *potentia* indicating the emergence of a second great awakening.

Throughout history, this awakening was navigated by initiation and rites of passage ceremony. The elements of initiation included:

- awakening from the conventional slumber and the departure from the known
- the journey into the unknown facing its ordeals and challenges (with guides and helpers providing wisdom and training)
- the transformation
- the journey back with its ordeals and challenges

- the return to the community—being received with a new status, recognition, and purpose

Boys are no longer removed from the village by the elder men, initiated and returned to the village as young men. But, the developmental necessity has not changed. The stage of initiation now is the family (and the larger community), and the boys are calling to their parents (and other adults) to engage and initiate them into young manhood. A fourteen-year-old told this story:

> I had a great childhood with wonderful parents who loved me. I don't know what happened but I got up on my fourteenth birthday, walked into the living room and discovered my parents were completely different. I couldn't stand them!

The boy's parents didn't change. He "woke up" from his conventional childhood world and "crossed the bridge" and entered the unknown world of adolescence. The "problems" that appeared, the conflicts, challenges, and ordeals that occurred, signaled that something new and different was happening. But now his parents were called to engage in the rite of passage with him, to be immersed in the challenges and ordeals created by conflict and resistance to the "rules of the realm," to co-empower his transformation and to welcome him into the fold with his rightful new status as a young man.

This is the challenge for the adults: to transcend their conventional roles and evolve into the wisdom-guide parents. When the "problems" become the focus of the adults' attention, when control battles and win/lose games are the activities they're engaged in, the opportunity for the creative evolution, the coming-into-being, of boys' young manhood, is lost. They're all mired down in rebellious battles that have no growth potential. Everybody loses.

This is not what the boys are calling for! They are calling for a loving understanding and acceptance of the world of teenage boys, especially the fundamental fact that they are trying to become young men. They are at the threshold of developing their freedom of choice and their independence: to be able to leave home to become their own men in the world fulfilling their destiny. They need their parents to recognize this fundamental fact and to help them.

Helping them requires parents to grow in their understanding and expression of power, conflict, and love. For dragons to develop self-confidence, self-regulation, and self-direction, they have to engage with parents and other adults who model the presence of power as self-mastery, conflict as a necessary creative process, and love as an embodied, all-inclusive, ever-present force in the relationship. For the boys to become courageous in the face of adversity and challenge, they must engage with adults who grow and change themselves in meeting the conflicts occurring with the boys. To come into their own, to develop inner strength, perseverance, and resilience, the boys have to work hard to acquire what they want, to sacrifice and give of themselves to obtain their goals, and be in service to the relationships. To develop trust and risk change themselves, the boys must be able to rely on their parents to embody an unconditional love and acceptance, to hold their space, act with integrity, and to keep their word. Finally, for their souls to awaken to their purposes in being, to begin to unfold into the future as the men they were born to become, the boys must journey and meet the challenges of making dreams come true, and be treated with respect, gravity, and seriousness by their parents in helping them on their paths. All of this is the contemporary context of initiation and rite of passage.

There is more of a need for power as control and domination, conflict as a contest with winners and losers, when a boy is a little: the hierarchical family structure has to be established in real time and space. *Once it is established* and the boy has reached the phase of development where he has to initiate his independence and he has to resist the "rule" of the hierarchical structure (authority of father and mother) to develop his autonomy, it *does not work* to re-assert control and domination in a "contest" to "defeat" him into obedience and conformity. He needs a *greater Love*—a love that comes from the parents' self-confidence in their authority *and* their recognition that their son is a soul unfolding, a person in his own right, emerging right before their eyes. They must adapt and develop their parenting to make room for his coming-into-being to occur. This is how "dragons" are "tamed." It is the path to his young manhood. It is the alchemy of parenting a teenage boy.

About the Author

Ted Braude is the director of the BoysWork Project. A graduate of the Merrill-Palmer Institute in Detroit, Michigan, he is a therapist, mentor, martial artist, musician, and writer who brings boys into young manhood. He has worked with boys and their families for over thirty years, and conducted training groups with boys; he has consulted with schools in developing boy-friendly education programs, supervised their staffs, and trained their boys. He has presented workshops and programs for boys, parents, educators, youth assistance workers, librarians, criminal justice personnel, and other professionals. He lives and works in Royal Oak, Michigan.

www.tedbraude.com